TECH-SAVVY

Educating Girls in the New Computer Age

By the AAUW Educational Foundation Commission on Technology, Gender, and Teacher Education

This report was made possible, in part, by the generous contribution of Margaret Strauss Kramer. Special thanks to the Northern Palm Beach Branch of AAUW.

Published by the American Association of University Women Educational Foundation
1111 Sixteenth Street N.W.
Washington, DC 20036
202/728-7602
Fax: 202/872-1425
TDD: 202/785-7777
foundation@aauw.org
www.aauw.org

First printing: April 2000
Cover design by Sabrina Meyers
Layout by Vann Dailly

Library of Congress Card Number: 00-100922
ISBN 1879922231

Cover photos: The Concord Consortium; Jeff Leaf; Judy Rolfe

Printed on
recycled paper

TABLE OF CONTENTS

FOREWORD

As the third millennium dawns, we know that computer technology has profoundly changed what we learn, how we learn it, and how we apply that learning in the workplace and throughout our lives. It is far less certain that all of us—or even most of us—are equipped to take full advantage of this technology.

Clear evidence that girls and women lag in interest and participation prompted the formation in 1998 of the AAUW Educational Foundation Commission on Technology, Gender, and Teacher Education. *Tech-Savvy: Educating Girls in the New Computer Age* represents the findings of this commission.

How do we educate girls to become tech-savvy women? The question facing the commission at its outset was an important one, and one to which this report devotes considerable attention. But by the end of the commissioners' year of collaborative study, they found themselves asking an equally compelling question: What changes are needed in the computer culture to improve its image, repair its deficits, and make it more appealing to girls and women?

These changes, commissioners increasingly understood, may also make technology more inviting to other underrepresented users—groups such as Hispanics, African Americans, low-income students, and students who do not identify with the "male hacker/computer geek" stereotype of the proficient technology user. This report explores how to make the defining technology of this century more accessible, appealing, and inviting to a variety of users and learners.

For women and girls, making the computer culture more reflective of their interests and values depends on their ability to influence the popular discourse about cyberculture and education. Many valid criticisms of computer culture by teachers and female students serve as useful counterbalances to the rampant technophilia of our age.

Goals, for example, need to be re-examined. Is simply getting more girls into computer science classes an adequate measure of success? Not for the commissioners. Clearly, they have much broader, much longer-term results in mind. For them, success is a commitment to lifelong technology learning, with all that that implies: an ability to adapt to rapid changes, interpret critically the wealth of electronic information, experiment without fear, and assume a variety of roles beyond that of end user or consumer.

In the classroom, commissioners want to see technology infused across the curriculum, to support better learning for all students in a variety of subject areas. This philosophy is especially crucial for equity questions. Girls and other nontraditional users of computer science—who are not enamored of technology for technology's sake—may be far more interested in using the technology if they encounter it in the context of a discipline that interests them.

Tech-Savvy is a timely contribution to make the information age serve all of our society.

Sharon Schuster
President
AAUW Educational Foundation
April 2000

EXECUTIVE SUMMARY

EXECUTIVE SUMMARY

In contemporary culture, the computer is no longer an isolated machine: It is a centerpiece of science, the arts, media, industry, commerce, and civic life. Information technology is transforming every field, and few citizens are unaffected by it. The commission has chosen to use the terms "computers" and "computer technology" to refer to this larger "e-culture" of information and simulation, and has focused its inquiries, discussion, and recommendations on computers and education.

The question is no longer whether computers will be in the classroom, but how computers can be used to enhance teaching and learning—ideally, in ways that promote the full involvement by girls and other groups currently underrepresented in many computer-related endeavors. The commission's themes and recommendations, while focused on girls in schools, would, if addressed, improve the quality of the computer culture for all students.

Key Themes

1. Girls have reservations about the computer culture—and with good reason. In its inquiries into gender issues in computers and education, the commission found that girls are concerned about the passivity of their interactions with the computer as a "tool"; they reject the violence, redundancy, and tedium of computer games; and they dislike narrowly and technically focused programming classes. Too often, these concerns are dismissed as symptoms of anxiety or incompetence that will diminish once girls "catch up" with the technology.

The commission sees it differently: In some important ways, the computer culture would do well to catch up with the girls. In other words, girls are pointing to important deficits in the technology and the culture in which it is embedded that need to be integrated into our general thinking about computers and education. Indeed, girls' critiques resonate with the concerns of a much larger population of reticent users. The commission believes that girls' legitimate concerns should focus our attention on changing the software, the way computer science is taught, and the goals we have for using computer technology.

2. Teachers in grades K-12 have concerns—and with good reason. Teachers, three-fourths of whom are women, critique the quality of educational software; the "disconnect" between the worlds of the curriculum, classroom needs, and school district expectations; and the dearth of adequate professional development and timely technical assistance. Even those teachers technologically savvy enough to respond to the commission's online survey had incisive criticisms of the ways that computer technology has come into the classroom, and of the ways that they are instructed and encouraged to use it.

Often, teachers' concerns are met with teacher bashing: "Teachers are not measuring up" to the new technology, is our frequent response. Again, the commission sees it differently. Rather than presume teachers' inadequacies, the commission believes that teachers need opportunities to design instruction that takes advantage of technology across all disciplines. Computing ought to be infused into the curriculum and subject areas that teachers care about in ways that promote critical thinking and lifelong learning.

3. Statistics on girls' participation in the culture of computing are of increasing concern, from the point of view of education, economics, and culture. Girls are not well-represented in computer laboratories and clubs, and have taken dramatically fewer programming and computer science courses at the high school and postsecondary level. Therefore, girls and women have been labeled as computer-phobic.

The commission sees it differently: It interprets such behavior not as phobia but as a choice that invites a critique of the computing culture. We need a more inclusive computer culture that embraces multiple interests and backgrounds and that reflects the current ubiquity of technology in all aspects of life. As this report describes, girls assert a "we can, but I don't want to" attitude toward computer technology: They insist on their abilities and skills in this area even as they vividly describe their disenchantment with the field, its careers, and social contexts. Although some of this attitude may be defensive, it is important to take a hard look at what these girls are feeling defensive about.

4. Girls' current ways of participating in the computer culture are a cause for concern. A common alternative to computer science courses—and a common point of entry for girls into the computer world—has been courses on computer "tools," such as databases, page layout programs, graphics, online publishing, and other "productivity software."

The commission believes that while mastery of these tools may be useful, it is not the same thing as true technological literacy. To be "technologically literate" requires a set of critical skills, concepts, and problem-solving abilities that permit full citizenship in contemporary e-culture. Girls' grasp of specific computer tools—use of the Internet and e-mail, and competency with productivity software such as PowerPoint or page layout programs—may have satisfied an older

standard of computer literacy and equity; the new definition of computer literacy and equity described in this report is a broader one. (See "What Is Fluency with Information Technology?" on page xi.)

The new standard of "fluency" assumes an ability to use abstract reasoning; to apply information technology in sophisticated, innovative ways to solve problems across disciplines and subject areas; to interpret vast amounts of information with analytic skill; to understand basic principles of programming and other computer science fundamentals; and to continually adapt and learn new technologies as they emerge in the future. It is our job as a society to ensure that girls are just as competent as their male peers in meeting these standards.

When they began their deliberations, commissioners explored various ways of defining what it would mean to achieve "gender equity" in the computer culture. Some commissioners emphasized concrete suggestions to get more girls into the "pipeline" to computer-related careers and to participate in these disciplines as they are presently constituted. Other commissioners emphasized ways that the computer culture itself could be positively transformed through the integration of girls' and women's insights, concentrating on the "web" of cultural associations that women's greater participation might create.

The commission does not view the two perspectives as dichotomous or competing. They are mutually reinforcing. One of the values in getting more girls and women in the computer pipeline is that their greater presence may transform the computer culture overall; by the same token, changes in the e-culture itself—the ways technology is discussed, valued, and applied—would invite more girls and women to participate fully in that culture.

What Is Fluency with Information Technology?

What "everyone should know" about technology cannot be a static list of prescriptions to use word processing programs or e-mail. Instead, fluency goals must allow for change, enable adaptability, connect to personal goals, and promote lifelong learning. Like language fluency, information technology fluency should be tailored to individual careers and activities.

As described by a National Research Council report, fluency with information technology* requires the acquisition of three kinds of interdependent knowledge that must be taught in concert: skills, concepts, and capabilities. Skills are necessary for job preparedness, productivity, and other aspects of fluency. They include such things as using the Internet to find information, or setting up a personal computer. Skills change as technology advances: Using the Internet became essential in the past five years, and designing a home page will be essential soon. Concepts explain how and why information technology works. Capabilities, essential for problem solving, include managing complex systems as well as testing solutions.

Fluency is best acquired when students do coherent, ongoing projects to achieve specific goals in subjects that are relevant and interesting to them.

A project for biology students might be: Design an information system to track HIV testing and notification; communicate the design to potential participants; and convince users that privacy will be maintained. In this example, students would need content knowledge about HIV testing and about notification practices. They would use fluency skills such as organizing a database and communicating with others, and fluency concepts such as algorithmic thinking and an understanding of personal privacy concerns. To complete the project, students would use fluency capabilities such as sustained reasoning, testing solutions, and communicating about information technology.

A project for German language learners might be: Critique a program that translates directions for using a cellular phone by researching alternative cellular phone interfaces; devise tests of the program; evaluate the translation with potential users; and design a presentation to communicate recommendations to program designers. Students would need content knowledge of contemporary German language, such as referring to a cellular phone as a "handy," as well as appreciation of the diverse cellular phone interfaces. Students would need fluency skills, such as using the Internet to find information and using a graphic or artwork package to create illustrations. They would use fluency concepts, such as algorithmic thinking and awareness of the social impact of information technology. To complete the project, they would use fluency capabilities, such as testing solutions, managing complex systems, and thinking about information technology abstractly.

* The term fluency and its description are adapted from the National Research Council, Computer Science and Telecommunications Board, *Being Fluent with Information Technology* (Washington, DC: National Academy Press, 1999).

The commission has reviewed existing research, considered research that the AAUW Educational Foundation commissioned on the topic, talked with researchers, and listened to girls' and teachers' observations about computing. The commissioners urge immediate action on the following recommendations to ensure social equity as well as a more thoughtful integration of technology in education and our lives.

KEY RECOMMENDATIONS

Compute across the curriculum. Computers can no longer be treated as a "set aside," lab-based activity. Computation should be integrated across the curriculum, into such subject areas and disciplines as art, music, and literature, as well as engineering and science. This integration supports better learning for all, while it invites more girls into technology through a range of subjects that already interest them.

Redefine computer literacy. Computer literacy needs to be redefined to include the lifelong application of relevant concepts, skills, and problem-solving abilities. What does this mean? Students must be trained to be literate citizens in a culture increasingly dependent on computers. Students—especially females, who predominate in clerical and service occupations—must be educated to move beyond word processing and presentation software to solve real-life problems with technology. While a tally of girls in computer science classes is a convenient benchmark, empowering girls and other nontraditional users to mine computer technology for sophisticated, innovative uses requires a mastery of these literacies and abilities, not quickly outdated programming skills alone. (See "What Is Fluency with Information Technology?" on page xi.)

Respect multiple points of entry. Different children will encounter different entry points into computing—some through art, for example, some through design, some through mathematics. These multiple entry points need to be respected and encouraged, while we remain sensitive to activities and perspectives that are appealing to girls and young women.

Change the public face of computing. Make the public face of women in computing correspond to the reality rather than the stereotype. Girls tend to imagine that computer professionals live in a solitary, antisocial, and sedentary world. This is an alienating—and incorrect—perception of careers that will rely heavily on computer technology and expertise in this century.

Prepare tech-savvy teachers. Schools of education have a special responsibility: They need to develop teachers who are able to design curricula that incorporate technology in a way that is inclusive of all students. Schools of education also must be able to assess "success" for students and teachers in a tech-rich classroom. The focus for professional development needs to shift from mastery of the hardware to the design of classroom materials, curricula, and teaching styles that complement computer technology.

Begin a discussion on equity for educational stakeholders. A more equitable and inclusive computer culture depends on consciousness-raising within schools about issues of gender, race, and class. School districts should put in place institutional mechanisms that will facilitate such conversations in partnership with parents, community leaders, and representatives from the computer and software industry.

Educate students about technology and the future of work. Schools have a message to communicate about the future of work: All jobs, including those in the arts, medicine, law, design, literature, and the helping professions, will involve more and more computing. Conversely, technological careers will increasingly draw on the humanities, social science, and "people skills." It is especially important that girls not bound immediately for college understand career options in computer and network support, and the impact of new technologies on more traditional fields.

Rethink educational software and computer games. Educational software and games have too often shown significant gender bias. Girls need to recognize themselves in the culture of computing. Software should speak to their interests and girls should be treated as early as possible as designers, rather than mere end users, of software and games.

Support efforts that give girls and women a boost into the pipeline. Create and support computing clubs and summer school classes for girls, mentoring programs, science fairs, and programs that encourage girls to see themselves as capable of careers in technology.

INTRODUCTION

Dual Visions

INTRODUCTION FROM THE COMMISSION

Dual Visions

In 1998 the AAUW Educational Foundation announced a 10-year research agenda that includes a focus on girls' and young women's educational preparation for an increasingly technological, information-driven economy. The AAUW Educational Foundation's report, *Gender Gaps,* had found cause for serious concern in the area of information technology. *Gender Gaps* reported alarming disparities in girls' and boys' enrollments in advanced computing courses. Girls were less likely to take high-level computing classes in high school, and comprised just 17 percent of those taking Advanced Placement computer science exams. Girls outnumbered boys only in their enrollment in word processing classes, arguably the 1990s version of typing. In 1995, at the postsecondary level, women received one in four of the computer/information science bachelor's degrees and only 11 percent of the doctorates in engineering-related technologies. These educational gaps reverberate in the workplace, where by most estimates women today occupy only 20 percent of the jobs in information technology.[1]

The AAUW Educational Foundation convened the Commission on Technology, Gender, and Teacher Education to make recommendations for research, practice, and policy that might address these gaps. The commission discussed the broad area of technology and gender equity and decided that it could make the most impact by focusing this report specifically on information technology. The commission, which met four times from November 1998 to January 2000, focused on educational experiences in K-12 public schools. The commission was co-chaired by Professor Sherry Turkle of MIT and Patricia Diaz Dennis of SBC Communications, and included participants from academia, education, business, and journalism. This report expresses the collective opinions and experiences of the commission, as well as findings from literature reviews and original research commissioned by the AAUW Educational Foundation. In particular, this report shares the voices of the girls who were interviewed in a qualitative study of 70 middle school and high school girls on the East Coast, and of the nearly 900 teachers nationwide who responded to an online survey commissioned by the Foundation.[2]

When they began their deliberations, commissioners explored various ways of defining what it would mean to achieve "gender equity" in the computer culture. Some commissioners focused on concrete suggestions to get more girls into the "pipeline" to computer-related careers and to participate in these disciplines and pursuits, as they are presently constituted.[3] Other commissioners emphasized ways that the computer culture itself could be positively transformed through the integration of girls' and women's insights.

The commission does not view the two perspectives as dichotomous or competing. They are mutually reinforcing. One of the values in getting more girls and women interested in the computer pipeline is that their greater presence may transform the computer culture overall; by the same token, changes in the e-culture itself—the ways technology is discussed, valued, and applied—would invite more girls and women to participate fully in that culture.

Both perspectives agree on the importance of making sure that girls and women are integrated into the computer culture throughout the range of occupations, and economic and social levels, whether they work as professionals or not. Computer fluency will benefit historians, architects, lawyers, and designers, as well as homemakers and blue-collar workers. Both perspectives share the goal of increasing literacy and technological fluency for girls and women—not simply as consumers or end users of technology, but as designers, leaders, and shapers of the computer culture.

Ultimately, the commission endorsed a dual vision of gender equity, in the following senses: First, it is desirable for more women to go into computer science and related technical disciplines (and to take the courses that would prepare them to do so); it is also desirable for more women to feel comfortable in the culture of computing, no matter what their eventual occupational, social, or family roles may be. The commission's criteria for technological fluency are demanding, but we believe they are realistic. In our view, fluency requires the ability to use technology proactively, understand design issues, and be able to interpret the information that technology makes available. It requires knowledge of how to choose software that serves one's needs, as well as the ability to evaluate materials on the World Wide Web. Perhaps most important, given the pace of technological change, fluency means becoming a lifelong learner of technology.

Second, the commission believes that in crucial ways what is "good for girls" would be good for all us. The commission believes that girls' experiences with computers in education speak to problems faced by a wider range of learners—girls and boys, men and women—as they encounter information technology.

The commission began with a directive to explore girls' underrepresentation in many areas of e-culture, consider avenues for further research, and suggest both short- and long-term recommendations that might improve the situation. This report contains recommendations that speak to this directive. But in the course of its deliberations, the commission came to recommendations that it believes would not only broaden girls' encounters with technology, but would stimulate a more inclusive computer culture for all students. Teachers and girls have concerns about the trajectory of the e-culture that need to be taken seriously, and they point to ways that computer technology could be more effectively and equitably taught to all students.

Third, we need to take account of both the complexity of the problem and the necessity and possibility for action and change. The issues demand humility: Subtle and numerous factors draw boys and girls, and men and women, toward different interests and career choices. Not surprisingly, boys and girls are drawn to different kinds of involvement with technology. Even the best recommendations and attendant policy decisions will face complex social and psychological obstacles. Additionally, because of the pace of change in this field, any unduly specific recommendations will become dated. And yet we are also optimistic: We believe that there are significant ways in which academic, educational, media, and business leaders can act collaboratively to make timely and effective change.

—*The AAUW Educational Foundation Commission on Technology, Gender, and Teacher Education*

CHAPTER 1

"WE CAN,
BUT I DON'T WANT TO":
Girls' Perspectives
on the Computer Culture

"WE CAN, BUT I DON'T WANT TO"

Girls' Perspectives on the Computer Culture

In this report, we use the terms "computer culture" or "e-culture" to refer not only to the computer that does things for us but to the computer that does thing to us as people, to our ways of relating to others and our ways of seeing the world.[4] Computer culture refers to the social, psychological, educational, and philosophical meanings associated with information technology. And we argue that the computer culture, or the technological mystique, can have a significant and negative impact on education. The cultural emphasis on technical capacity, speed, and efficiency when discussing computers estranges a broad array of learners, many girls included, who do not identify with the wizardry of computer aficionados and have little interest in the purely technical aspects of the machines. As commission co-chair Sherry Turkle writes, the computer culture has become linked to a characteristically masculine worldview, such that women too often feel they need to choose between the cultural associations of "femininity" and those of "computers."[5]

Girls who participated in focus groups commissioned by the AAUW Educational Foundation give voice to the contradictions and tensions in the computer culture. They almost never report overt discrimination: They were not told directly that they were less competent with technology than boys, nor were they openly deterred from enrolling in computer courses. But at the same time, when asked to describe a person who is "really good with computers," they describe a man. And most of them do not predict that they will want to learn more about or become more involved with computers in the future. In Turkle's terms, these girls are not computer-phobic; they are "computer reticent." They say that they are not afraid but simply do not want to get involved. They express a "we can, but I don't want to" philosophy.

Strikingly, girls' views of computer careers, and of the computer culture—including software, games, and Internet environments—tend to reproduce stereotypes about a "computer person" as male and antisocial, a cliché that has proven resistant to the growing diversity of information technology and its users. Even if we assume that some of the resolve behind the "we don't want to" attitude is defensive, it is important to understand what girls are defensive about, and to take seriously their critiques of the computer culture.

Stereotypes: Ambivalence and Contradictions

In focus groups, most girls took offense at any suggestion that there may be differences in how boys and girls interact with computers. "[It's not boys or girls,] it's just personality," a Fairfax, Virginia, girl summarizes. Another participant emphatically states, "You can't base it on the sex. It's the kind of person." And girls readily affirm that women and men have equal aptitude in the area of computing. However, in the same conversations, while rejecting generalizations about gender in the abstract, girls reveal a highly developed set of beliefs about how boys and girls differ in their relationship to computer technology. In other words, we found that girls observe and describe strong gender differences but do not have a language with which to talk about them. The result is that girls are likely to express bewilderment and confusion about how they are different in their attitudes and abilities than boys. In girls' efforts to find a perspective from which to talk about gender differences, they often position themselves as morally or socially more evolved than boys who, they tell us, enjoy "taking things apart" and interacting with "machines."

Guys are more interested in taking apart things. It's part of their nature to do more electrical stuff than girls. They like to brag.

—Baltimore high school student

As most girls present it, their more limited involvement with computers, especially their lack of interest in games and their lack of interest in having a career in computing, has more to do with disenchantment than with anxiety or intellectual deficiency. They say that girls are engaged with the world, while boys are engaged with computers. One high school girl brands boys' relationships to computers as childish: "Immature. They just get worked up ... they spend all their time on computers and they just never grow." Girls return repeatedly to a criticism that computers (which they particularly associate with Internet cruising and games) are a "waste of time." As a Fairfax middle school girl remarks, "I don't usually go on the Internet with my friends. I think that I have better things to do with them."

Girls have other priorities. Guys are more computer-type people.

—Fairfax, Virginia, middle school student

Disenchantment, Not Phobia

Girls discuss information technology-related careers not as too difficult, but as a "waste of intelligence" and, in some cases, materialistic and shortsighted.

(See "The Work Environment" section in Chapter 5, "The School in Context.") Insists a Baltimorean, "Guys just like to do that: sit in a cubicle all day." One girl imagines she might "think about doing it as a starting off thing just to get some money," but once she had the money, she would "go into something that I actually enjoy."

Girls describe gender differences most vividly in relation to the Internet and computer games. (See Chapter 3, "Educational Software and Games.") They tend to present the Internet as a vice in the hands of boys, and a virtue in the hands of girls, because boys use it to play games and "fool around" while girls use it as a source of information. When asked to draw two boys talking about computers, one girl depicts "two guys saying, 'Dude, check it out. Let's go look at some pics of Pamela Anderson.' And the other one is like, 'Let's go to the virtually-kill-a-Teletubbie website.'" A group of high school girls in Fairfax, Virginia, was adamant that girls are more able than boys to resist the negative influences of computer culture. One student says: "I think once we [girls] have morals and ideas about something, we can't really be affected by a computer game. I think there might be some people out there who are very weak-minded and when they see that, they go out [and do it.] Boys are, just in general, more violent." The Richmond group of middle school girls said that video games are more likely to capture boys' interest than girls' because "we have a better social life"; "we probably want to chat and they just want to play something"; and, interestingly, "it gives them artificial power that they feel is important."

Girls have specific criticisms of the violence in current games as well as the general sense that they would be more interested in games that allowed them to create rather than destroy. When given the opportunity to describe their "ideal" computer game, they talk about how they would value games that involve simulation and identity play. They would appreciate opportunities to "work through" real-life problems in the simulated world of the screen. Many describe games that would allow them to swap identity or face struggles they have yet to encounter.

The Tool/Toy Divide

The focus groups support a recurrent theme in research on gender and technology: Girls approach the computer as a "tool" useful primarily for what it can do; boys more often view the computer as a "toy" and/or an extension of the self (what Turkle has called the projective qualities of the computer, the computer as "Rorschach" or "second self"). For boys, the computer is inherently interesting. Girls are interested in its instrumental possibilities, which may include its use as an artistic medium. They express scorn toward boys who confuse "real" power and power on a screen. "I see a computer as a tool," a high school girl declares. "You [might] go play Kung Fu Fighting, but in real life you are still a stupid little person living in a suburban way."

> ### I try not to have emotions about inanimate objects.
>
> —Washington, DC, high school student

Because they want to use computers to get things done, girls tend to deem them "boring unless I'm using them for my own purposes." They tend to equate understanding the inner workings of the computer with boys' tendency to be interested in technology for its own sake, something that does not, in the main, capture girls' interests. With sarcasm, a student in Baltimore narrates her sketch of two boys "talking about how [a new program] is going to take all my memory because it takes like 200,000 megabytes, or whatever."

> ### Women are more interested in what they have to get done and men just want to play around.
>
> —Baltimore middle school student

While girls in the focus groups show little interest in the inner workings of the computer, they are very interested in the possibilities of using technology to promote human interaction. Says a Richmond middle school student, "Girls use [the computer] more for communication to their friends. I always like to talk to people online, and my brother just plays games." When they are asked to describe girls and computers, most depict girls talking about talking—asking whether they received the latest e-mail, or assessing the merits of chat rooms. Although these activities may conform to stereotypes about girls' cultures, focus group participants nonetheless see them as more valuable interactions with technology than the machine-centered activities they observe boys to favor.

Girls in the focus groups explain that building human relationships is as intellectually complex and valuable as understanding machines; they question boys' absorption with computers as a substitute for social skills. As one high school student put it, "Women are into talking to each other and building these relationships, and guys—they are not as comfortable with themselves or with each other. They just like to build a relationship by putting it into the computer."

These girls' descriptions of what boys are doing with technology are missing some very important elements. There is strong value in boys' activities that girls are quick to denigrate. For example, there is intellectual importance to getting to understand computers from the "inside out" and developing skills and an intuitive feel for programming. There is intellectual value in tinkering with technology. And there is no question that there is defensiveness in the way girls denigrate these activities. But it is also clear that getting girls involved with computing will require overcoming resistance based on their negative feelings about getting involved with the machine "for itself." This resistance also stems from girls' view that a machine-centered, technical worldview is what the computer culture is all about. Girls reject a computer culture that they see as primarily focused on playing with machines.

However, girls in these groups resist the cliché that they do not "like" computers. Rather, they clarify that there are multiple ways of "liking" computer technology. One girl explains as follows the persistence of this cliché: "Girls," she says, "don't talk about computer stuff as much as guys do. That might give people the opinion that we don't like it as much or anything, but we just don't talk about it." Girls insist that they like computers; they just "like them for different things."

Girls' descriptions of computer culture reproduce some powerful, enduring clichés about what it means to work with computers that appear out of step with recent events and developments. The clichés are about social isolation and an exclusive focus on the machine. In fact, computer work and human-computer interaction today is diverse. Much of it centrally involves understanding and interacting with people in complex social systems. In order to attract girls and women to computing, we need to broaden the meanings and values associated with technology and technological work.

KEY RECOMMENDATIONS

To the Media:
• **Change the public face of computing.** Girls tend to imagine that computer professionals live in a solitary, antisocial, and sedentary world. This is an alienating—and incorrect—perception of the kind of careers that are available in the computer culture. And girls complain that they do not see women in the media who are actively involved in computing. One solution is to use popular girls' media to promote real women doing work using computer technology. The goal of this campaign would be to change the entrenched stereotype of the "computer person" as male and socially isolated.

• Increase the visibility of women who have taken the lead in designing and using computer technology. Girls express an interest in seeing such women, who have often not become public figures.

• Highlight the human, social, and cultural dimensions and applications of computers, rather than the technical advances, the speed of the machines, or the entrepreneurial culture surrounding them.

To Parents, Students, Educators, Software Designers, and School Districts:
• **Start the conversation about gender in the computer culture.** A more equitable and inclusive computer culture depends on consciousness-raising within schools about issues of gender, race, and class. It will be useful to discuss gender differences about computing and the computer culture. This conversation must take seriously girls' and women's valid critiques of computer design, use, and applications.

• **Invite girls into the "tinkering" aspects of computation.** These activities are crucially important for empowering women as designers and builders, not just consumers and end users. Tinkering activities should emphasize the pleasures of experimentation and creative, "artistic" play. Tinkering with code need not be seen as less artistic than tinkering with color, form, and shape. The fact that it is seen as such depends in large part on the way our culture has "constructed" mathematics, science, and computer science as uncreative. This perception can and should be changed.

CHAPTER 2

IN THE SCHOOL:

Teacher Perspectives

and

Classroom Dynamics

IN THE SCHOOL

Teacher Perspectives and Classroom Dynamics

Issues of gender equity in computing take place against the general background of an educational system that has significant gaps in its technological infrastructure. According to a 1998 National Science Foundation-sponsored report by Henry Becker and Ronald Anderson, only 25 percent of all U.S. K-12 schools qualified as "technology intensive" by meeting these "undemanding" criteria: 1) a student/computer ratio no higher than six to one; and 2) at least one-quarter of these computers able to run CD-ROMs for multimedia applications or provide moderate to high-speed Internet access.[6]

The most significant gaps in the distribution of computing resources are based on community income. Only 16 percent of schools in low-income communities have high-speed Internet access, for example, compared to 37 percent of schools in higher-income communities. A 1999 national survey of 1,000 public schools found that in poorer schools—those where 71 percent or more of students are eligible for free or reduced-cost lunch—only 39 percent of classrooms had any Internet access. School differences by race were relatively inconsequential compared to income; differences of metropolitan status (urban, suburban, or rural schools), type of school (public or private), and region were low or nonexistent, although the South tends to lag behind other areas of the country on most indicators.[7]

The most recent national survey of 1,400 teachers finds that although 97 percent of teachers report using computers at home or at school for professional work, not as many use computers in classroom instruction. Sixty-one percent of those surveyed use the Internet in class, and 53 percent use computer software. Seventy-five percent cite a shortage of computers in the classroom as a major obstacle. Only 5 percent of the teachers with one or two computers in the classroom say they use software and the Internet to "a very great extent," compared to 20 percent with six or more machines.[8]

Why don't teachers use computer technology more? Reasons go beyond the very real problems of technical infrastructure. One of the most striking findings of the Foundation's survey work with teachers is that many of the teachers technologically "savvy" enough to complete an online survey see little reason to use computer technology in their classroom work. One-third of teachers surveyed report frequent use, and one-quarter report regular use. Even technologically competent teachers are not persuaded that current educational applications can help their students. Teachers, like students, have their own version of computer reticence. We now turn to its sources.

PROFESSIONAL DEVELOPMENT AND TEACHER EDUCATION

The commission noted that putting technology into schools has usually come before teachers have been introduced to ways to use it, and has certainly preceded any discussion of social equity and technology. This pattern needs to be reversed, and the coming infusion of an estimated two million new teachers into the public school system this decade creates a rich opportunity to do so.[9]

K-12 public education is one of the more prominent "pink collar" occupations, employing three women to each man. Realistically, the question of teacher education becomes an issue that must be highly sensitive to issues of gender. But research on educational technology has too often treated teachers as an undifferentiated population. Teachers' concerns about technology use echo women's greater skepticism about technology's ability to solve complex social problems. They also echo women's lack of interest in understanding technology "for itself." Commissioner Cornelia Brunner notes that these perspectives "can be seen as a healthy counterbalance to a more masculine technophilia" in K–12 education, yet they are generally absent in the discussion of teacher education and technology. Research emphasizes that teachers play a critical role in how computers are integrated in the classroom. Hence it is important to take seriously educators' insights, concerns, and goals.[10]

I envision that most of our teaching techniques will have to change to fully incorporate computers and technology. Older teachers are afraid to work with computers because there has been very little meaningful training.

—teacher survey, on the future of the classroom

Studies of preservice teachers find high levels of anxiety about technology and little knowledge or experience with how to use it other than for word processing or administrative tasks.[11] More innovative uses of technology in education have only rarely been emphasized in teacher education and professional development programs.[12]

Education schools tend to give instruction in basic technical skills rather than on how to integrate computers into the curriculum. A 1999 national survey found that only 29 percent of teachers had six or more hours of curriculum-integration instruction, whereas 42 percent had that amount of basic-skills training. Of the 892 "high end" teachers polled for this research, only 267 (30 percent) report that they received any technology training in an undergraduate or master's teacher education program; this probably reflects, in part, responses from older teachers. Only 11 percent of the total respondents report that they received training specifically in how to apply or integrate computer technology into their lesson plans. Thus, current practices emphasize what researcher Linda Darling-Hammond has called a "drive by" approach, emphasizing short technical courses on connectivity and hardware. Preservice teachers make it clear that they start their jobs uninformed about what the technology is supposed to accomplish for their classrooms, either educationally or socially.[13]

The "drive by" approach to teacher training focuses on the technical properties of hardware; it does not emphasize educational applications or innovative uses of computing across the curriculum. Yet research suggests that what teachers need is sustained and ongoing education about how to integrate technology with curricular materials and information about how to make technology part of a humanistic classroom culture. This latter approach would create better-informed teachers as well as multiple entry points to computer competence for both students and teachers. The prevailing emphasis on the "mechanics of computer operation" does not respond to this need.[14]

Without teacher education, it won't matter if each student has his/her own computer. I do believe we are headed in the direction of better training for teachers. That will be the key. We teachers hate having thousands of dollars of equipment thrown at us and being told to use it when we have no clue how to go about it.

—teacher survey, on the future of the classroom

The commission recommends overall that professional development focus on designing effective uses for technology across the curriculum. Professional development, both preservice and inservice, needs to emphasize more than the use of the computer as a productivity tool. It must give teachers enough understanding of how computer technology works so that they feel like empowered users. It must also address how this dynamic and changing resource can be adapted, redesigned, and applied to advance the dual goals of better and more equitable instruction in all subject areas and disciplines.

Designing professional development for better instruction and equity demands comprehensive, not piecemeal, efforts. It might include:

• *Disseminating exemplary cases of teaching equity and excellence in the technology-rich classroom.*

• *Encouraging innovative course design as well as opportunities for ongoing reflection.* It is unreasonable to expect change from one-hour workshops on equity and technology, which are typically "quick fixes" rather than genuine occasions to transform the learning environment and teaching approach.[15]

• *Advancing fluency among teachers.* Teachers need opportunities to develop their own understanding of the strengths and limitations of technology by participating in collaborative efforts to design applications or customize flexible software. They need to understand the value of design of software for educational benefit. They need some sense of how the economics and politics of the mass media form and inform educational products.[16]

• *Showing tangible benefits.* Teachers need to see tangible and feasible benefits for using technology, and are less impressed by abstractions about the power of computer technology.

• *Spending time on classroom dynamics.* Teacher educators need to integrate discussions of classroom management, student interactions, and other contextual issues into discussions of teaching in the wired classroom.

• *Teaching contingencies for the technology-rich lesson plan.* Computer technology cannot and should not replace the range of instructional materials used in a multimedia classroom. How does computer technology mesh with other instructional materials and teaching strategies? These issues belong just as much in "technology education" as teaching familiarity with machinery.

TEACHERS' VIEWS OF COMPUTER LITERACY

In the United States, there is a broad-based conviction that computer technology belongs in all K-12 classrooms, but proponents are often unclear about the rationale behind the conviction. Why should computer technology occupy a central and privileged place in the 21st-century curriculum for public schools? And if it is to be central, how will we know if its deployment has achieved gender and social equity? How will we measure gender equity in the computer age?

Commissioners agree that an emphasis on "tools" (such as teaching students how to use word processing programs or presentation software) is not sufficient to support meaningful change in how or what students learn. Additionally, they agree that for technology to support better learning, it needs to be infused across the K-12 curriculum. It cannot be confined, as is too often the case, to a specific school location (the computer lab), a discrete set of skills (programming), or a discrete discipline (computer

Teachers' Attitudes

Computers, in one teacher's phrase, "are here to stay." Resoundingly, both male and female teachers surveyed for this report feel that the importance of computer technology will "increase significantly" in the next decade (76 percent), with an additional 21 percent answering that it will "increase somewhat." A small percentage (3 percent) feel the importance will "stay the same," but only eight respondents among 900 think it will decrease even somewhat. When asked to judge the prevalence of certain attitudes toward computer-assisted learning among colleagues at their school, teachers rate "It's an exciting, increas-ingly important teaching tool" as "somewhat common" (51 percent) or even "very common" (20 percent). The view that computer technology "is a fad—this too shall pass" they rank as "very uncommon" (43 percent). However, teachers are not uniformly sanguine about computers in the classroom: Roughly one in three teachers surveyed deem it a "very common" or "somewhat common" attitude that computers are an "unpleasant but necessary part of teaching nowadays" (36 percent), a "time-consuming obstacle" (35 percent), or a "'crutch,' useful for entertainment value" (32 percent).

Teacher Attitudes Toward Technology

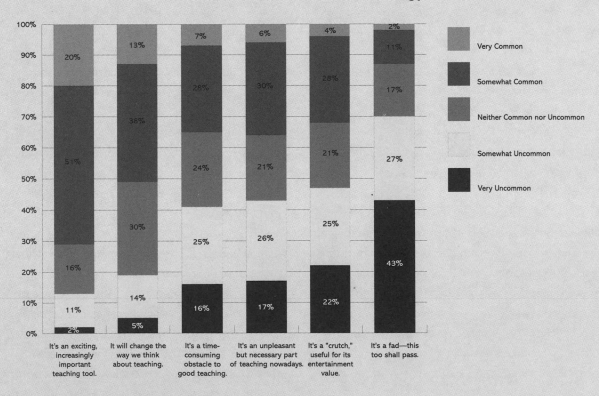

Source: Harris Online Survey, AAUW Educational Foundation, 1999

Teachers' Feelings About Technology

Personally, the majority of tech-savvy teachers surveyed feel "excited" (46 percent) and "empowered" (30 percent of men, 36 percent of women) about computer technology in the classroom, with female teachers more likely to say they feel "excited," "empowered," and "challenged" (38 percent of women and 25 percent of men). Very few teachers, either male or female, feel "cynical," "skeptical," or "confused" (3 percent or under for each).

In their descriptions of the future of the classroom, teachers often describe computer technology as an inevitable, if ambiguous, centerpiece of 21st-century education. Some teachers express resignation toward the high-tech classroom of the 21st century, and one group fears its own obsolescence. "Computers will probably replace me," one teacher speculates, and another fears that "sadly, education will eventually be taken over by computers. And teachers will just be in the room to supervise." These worries reveal a perhaps not uncommon assumption among teachers and others that computers are disembodied from human and social contexts, and, in effect, "do" things on their own.

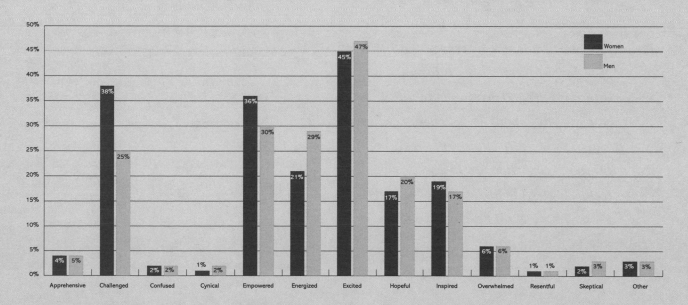

Which of the following words most closely characterizes your feelings about the technology-rich classroom?

Note: Respondents could chose up to two answers.

Source: Harris Online Survey, AAUW Educational Foundation, 1999

science). There are, however, many commissioners who feel strongly that girls' and women's underrepresentation in classes in programming and computer science at both the high school and postsecondary level is a serious problem. These commissioners stress that women's empowerment in the computer culture—to head design teams, lead organizations, and create new meanings and uses for technology—demands that they come to the table with a full range of technical skills. Women's participation in technical disciplines is important, but—in keeping with the commission's dual vision—we also stress that computing across the curriculum has deep value and will go a long way toward integrating diversity into the computer culture.

> *Learning is no more about the computer than it is about a pencil. But, in saying that, I must qualify… it isn't just a "tool." The computer has profoundly changed the way we interact with information. … So we must change the way we teach. Information is not learning, and the process of transforming information into knowledge/learning is what education is about. …Teachers need to understand more about how learning takes place if they are to use technology to facilitate that learning. What do we want students to know and be able to do?*
>
> —teacher survey, on the future of the classroom

Not many teachers are at a point where they have the wherewithal or luxury to think about computing across the curriculum. In the main, they are working with a set of less ambitious models. Many teachers surveyed hold a "productivity" model about the use of computers in education, which predicts a change in the quantity and reliability of computer technology, but few changes in what is taught (the curriculum) and how it is taught (pedagogy). They are trying to mesh computer technology into traditional lesson plans, subject areas, classroom protocols, and instructional formats (lectures). For example, some teachers imagine computer technology as a more efficient way to deliver lectures and textbook material in a whole-class instruction format: "I want the computer to become my blackboard," a teacher writes, "where I can call up multiple screens. … This way students can see anything I am saying."[17]

> *Each child has his/her own computer, on which all written work is done. [I envision] special classes for children whose technical skill is on a par with the rest of the group. [I envision] all testing done on computer on floppy disk, which is handed in for correction, thus effecting a wonderful saving of paper and time.*
>
> —teacher survey, on the future of the classroom

In a productivity model, "gender equity" in computer technology might mean girls' comparable mastery of tools such as PowerPoint, e-mail, Internet research and information retrieval, word processing, and databases. To a large extent, most girls and women already have demonstrated a familiarity with these specific tools and functions. But this alone has not worked in their favor: The majority of low-paying word processing and data processing jobs in the service, clerical, and retail industries are held by women, and women now use e-mail and the Internet in equal numbers to men. But women are dramatically underrepresented in information technology

(IT) jobs, systems analysis, software design, programming, and entrepreneurial roles.[18]

Many teachers surveyed by the commission hold a second view of computers in the school that emphasizes career preparation. The "career" view of computer technology holds that the future classroom will need to impart more complex computer skills to students to equip them for jobs. Almost all teachers surveyed (96 percent) agree strongly or somewhat that they would use computer technology in the classroom because "it is a necessary skill for students to learn," and because it "prepares students for the world of work" (93 percent). This view of the computer presents technology as a subject within the curriculum, taught in order to equip students for the job market of this century. "For a student to compete in the world of work," a teacher summarizes, "it is essential that he or she be able to use computers." Teachers who view education from a job market perspective emphasize that high schools will have to offer a "computer-savvy" foundation in order for students to compete and meet economic needs.

From the career perspective, "gender equity" might be interpreted to mean that as many girls as boys are skilled in computer applications required for professional jobs in the next century. It might also define gender equity more ambitiously as a parity of girls and boys in specific areas of the curriculum such as computer science and programming, where girls are currently underrepresented.[19]

We turn now to the fluency model of computers in education, the model that the commission finds most promising. It is championed by a smaller group of teachers surveyed, a group that we believe it is important to support. These teachers hope that in the future, technology-rich classrooms will promote more active learning that will emphasize problem-solving and critical thinking. They hope that technological skill-sets will be utilized and applied across the curriculum to present meaningful real-life problems for students to solve. The infusion of technology across the curriculum has particular relevance for equity, because it interweaves learning technologies into a variety of subjects and disciplines that already engage girls and other learners not drawn to computer technology for its own sake.[20]

Computers will not be a separate instruction; they will be integrated into all aspects of instruction.

—teacher survey, on the future of the classroom

Teacher advocates of the fluency model tend to imagine that the K-12 curriculum will be changed through greater access to information and more potential for individualized, self-paced curriculum. They also believe that pedagogy might change through access to classrooms, experts, other students, and teachers at remote sites. One teacher envisions that "students will be more aware of the global picture, and the information available to them will be far more intensive."

Put simply, the teacher will move from the "sage on the stage" to the "guide on the side," and students will use thinking and learning skills and have knowledge of these processes. Ideally, all children will have a laptop, and this will enable them to bridge the gap between home and school. ...[There will be] greater motivation because of empowerment of the students. [Schools will] need to work cooperatively and collaboratively in tune with the needs of ... the next millennium.

—teacher survey, on the future of the classroom

Another imagines global problem-solving-based education, with "classrooms around the world working on common problems and goals. ... I see a lessening of the emphasis on rote 'drill and practice' type lesson and an increased emphasis on higher level, more abstract problem-solving activities."

An optimistic teacher writes that "the computer can literally bring the world into one classroom, leading to more united, peaceful, tolerant, intelligent children." A more modest version of this projection is that "students could do comparative studies [and] have a broader perspective on the differences we have in this world."

> *I like watching students find the connection in all curriculum areas with assistance from this technology. [I like] knowing that my students will understand that change is inevitable and are prepared to learn new technology. [I like] knowing my students do not fear technology and understand that it is woven into every aspect of their lives.*
>
> —teacher survey, on the "best moment" with computer technology

The fluency view of technology in the classroom suggests a complex set of standards for "success" in achieving gender equity. It focuses attention on girls' abilities to use computers to engage in imaginative, creative, and improvised solutions to problems. Commissioner Marcia Linn draws attention to the ways in which this perspective on technological fluency resembles the standards for "fluency with information technology (FITness)" established by the National Research Council. These standards expect, among other things, that students:

- understand information technology broadly enough to apply it at work and in their everyday lives;

- continually adapt to changes in technology and improvise solutions when systems do not act in anticipated ways;

- apply insights about technology across domains and problems;

- understand basic concepts of programming and human-computer interfaces;

- interpret and understand information available through computer technology;

- define complex problems and imagine ways that information technology might contribute to the solution;

- think about information technology abstractly; and

- communicate effectively to others about it.[21]

The Foundation's commission believes that teachers, of course, should be able to use computers as tools, and that girls and women do need to be prepared to compete in the economy. But it also believes that an educational system that takes computer fluency as its goal holds the greatest promise for the achievement of meaningful gender equity in the computer culture. Girls and women should be prepared to become life-long learners, capable of thinking critically and abstractly about how to apply information technology to solve real-life problems.

RECOMMENDATIONS

Infuse technology across disciplines and subject areas. Advocate technology as a learning partner across the curriculum. This strategy is important for improving learning, developing computer literacy, and inviting a variety of users, including girls, into technology. The infusion of technology across the curriculum also recognizes and supports multiple entry points into technology. Some learners may develop a fluency with information technology through music, some through mathematics, and others through the arts.

Redefine "computer literacy." The commission noted that skills with literacy, numeracy, cognitive science, problem solving, analysis, and logic are as integral to computer expertise as a facility with machines and programming. The standard of gender equity in the computer culture should emphasize these characteristics of fluency. These characteristics are not about machines—they are about thinking.

Design for equity. Recommendations and guidelines for evaluating and refining the curriculum include the following:

Choose engaging and relevant subjects and undertakings. To attract girls and other "nontraditional" users to computer technology and other technologies, schools must allow students to engage in serious undertakings done in ways that are attractive to a diverse array of "types" and learners.

Develop more content applications. Teachers, curriculum developers, technology experts, and other stakeholders need to work together to create content applications that use technology to advance learning in particular subject areas. The content and technology link will further broaden the relevance of computer technology to groups of students not attracted to programming or computer science classes on their own terms.

Incorporate customizable technological learning environments in the classroom. Technology that can be personalized by students, updated, and reconstructed will be more inviting for students and less likely to become obsolete than stand-alone hardware.

Develop appropriate assessment tools. Assessment methods need to be appropriate to computer-assisted learning and the goals established for technology use. Rather than determine a curricular list of topics or benchmarks that girls "need to know" to be successful in computing—benchmarks that will become quickly obsolete as new programming tools and languages develop—time would be better spent investigating how to promote lifelong learning. Girls especially, who now predominate in word processing classes, need to know how to teach themselves about technology to become more adept at learning, critical thinking, and problem solving throughout their lives.

TEACHERS' APPREHENSIONS: "MANAGING" THE TECHNOLOGY-RICH CLASSROOM

Although many school districts are "getting wired" through hardware purchases and distribution, they are doing so even as they ignore the pedagogical, cultural, and social dynamics of classroom use.[22] Teachers, however, are very concerned about these matters, and their apprehensions need to be addressed systematically. First, teachers are concerned about managing technology-enriched classes. In particular, some express fears about maintaining

I wanted my students to get a good idea of the five themes of geography. I chose "traveling across the United States." The program was on a third-grade level, and required kids to find routes and mileage only. My students quickly caught on to the fact that I was a REAL computer novice. They would laugh each time I used a computer and wanted to know if I had the "age appropriate" program.

—teacher survey, on the "worst moment" with technology

their authority and the respect of their students in the wired classroom. It is understandable that these concerns may be particularly pronounced for older, female teachers, who are less likely to perceive themselves as experts. Some feel belittled in their roles as teachers by the mysterious and sometimes erratic presence of computer technology: "I have tried to avoid using technology," one wrote, "because 1) The administration sets it up and expects teachers to know how to use it without ongoing training—both in the technological AND curricular aspects, and 2) It is embarrassing to look incompetent in front of a roomful of fourth-grade students—particularly if a parent is in the room! Nonetheless, I usually press on and try to learn something from the kids, using the experience to emphasize that we need to think of ourselves as 'lifelong learners.'"

A "substitute teacher" was in my classroom and one of my students downloaded the "Bitch" song from the Southpark site [sic]. I didn't know it was there until a few days later when the principal was in my room and one of my students played it.

—teacher survey, on the "worst moment" with technology

Some teachers are concerned about their students accessing "porn" sites and other sexual material using the Internet, "even with the filters," and again, a great deal of teachers' anxiety seems to be about not being perceived as being in control or doing a good job. One teacher says: "I looked away and another teacher found one of my students in a pornographic site. The student was suspended for three days. I felt like I had not done my job."

In mixed-sex classrooms, especially, the use of information technology to reach sexually explicit or risqué text and material provides a high-tech medium for teasing, harassment, and embarrassment. From the teachers' perspective, the introduction of this material disrupts learning and weakens their confidence in being able to manage technology in the classroom.

I was introducing beginning Internet search skills. ... I gave my students permission to search for a rock band through Yahoo. While I was helping another student, I suddenly saw SEX flashing from the computer screen in 15-inch-high letters. Apparently this was a song title that was followed by the complete graphic lyrics.

—teacher survey, on the "worst moment" with technology

Commissioners concur that the use of technical safeguards and firewalls will not make this problem go away. Classrooms cannot rely solely on technical safeguards to make sexually explicit and hate sites disappear. As is clear from teachers' comments, students are already very much aware of the existence of these sites in cyberspace. As a way to advance media literacy, teachers should discuss openly these realities of cyberspace and why certain sites may be offensive to some people. Making students responsible for monitoring their own searches and avoiding inappropriate material is much more successful than relying on technical firewalls alone. In addition, agreements designed by many state education organizations enable students, parents, and teachers to jointly agree on acceptable behavior and consequences.

The Ideal: Computer Technology and the Inclusive Classroom

Roughly 15 percent of teachers describe a "best moment" with computer technology that promoted greater inclusion of all learners, learning styles, and more perspectives in their classrooms. Teachers report that even simple or basic uses of computer technology can level the playing field for students with physical or learning disabilities, limited English language ability, or deafness.

> *I currently work in an alternative school that has unmotivated students. I am so grateful that some of my students have started making web pages (which I don't know how to do) and are considering starting their own business. ...They really challenge themselves to be creative. ... I have also had the opportunity ... to produce two television-length commercials on environmental issues. Students were exposed to top-of-the-line equipment. They wrote, taped, produced, and edited (and played their own music for) a 30-second and a 60-second video that were televised as public service announcements. Both of these experiences have challenged my students with "real-life" problem solving—and they excelled.*

—teacher survey, on the "best moment" with computer technology

Teachers praise computers for enabling students of varying abilities and backgrounds to learn together "at their own pace." They report that remedial exercises are easier to accommodate with computer technology, and that students who "rarely succeed at conventional teaching methods not only succeed, but enjoy learning." A teacher fondly recalls "watching students accomplish tasks they thought were impossible. Students who were labeled slow learners were actually some of the best computer operators in the class and were able to help others complete projects."

Other teachers are enthusiastic that information technology allows them to customize the curriculum and to supplement the curriculum through the Internet to include information about groups that may get overlooked in traditional textbooks. As one teacher writes: "Students have been able to find information about Spanish/Hispanic artists of all eras that is simply not available in a traditional media center setting."

Single-Sex Classrooms?

The existing research base on gender and social relationships in technology-rich classrooms is small, and more study is needed. Commissioner Kathleen Bennett, who directs a technology-magnet middle school for girls, drew the commission's attention to the complexity of this issue. On the one hand, girls face a future in which they will work together with men. It makes sense to prepare them for this reality rather than protect them from it. On the other hand, some research suggests that boys and girls working together with computers means trouble for girls. An ethnographic study of first-grade students in 1998 found that females in mixed-sex groups were more likely to have their competence questioned; their work critiqued, laughed at, or publicly criticized; and their concentration interrupted by males than those working alone or in all-female groups. A 1999 qualitative study of 67 computer science students in the eleventh grade similarly found that girls in all-female environments perceived greater teacher support than either males or females in mixed-sex settings. Other research found that females performed better on a computer-based tracking task in the presence of another female as the "audience." Two studies found that all-female or majority-female groups of students cooperate substantially more on computer tasks than majority-male groups or mixed pairs. Regardless of group composition, females use a more inclusive language than males in discussing their work, and give constructive advice to boys more than the converse. It is important to note, however, that boys, although less likely to cooperate, show the greatest performance gains when cooperating with other students. This dramatizes the fact that boys as well as girls will profit from changes in classroom computer culture that are focused on equity.[23]

> *Girls seem to work better together and in all-female groups. Boys like to work more on their own and "take over" if they work with girls.*
>
> —teacher survey, on gender and software

Teachers need to be vigilant in technology-rich classrooms. For example, if teachers allow students to select their own computer lab partners, this may encourage sex segregation. If teachers allow students to assign themselves roles in group work, this may encourage stereotyping by race or sex—that is, the girl plays the role of "secretary" or note-taker. Teachers might consider assigning and then frequently alternating roles in group work, and integrating oral and written communication skills into computer science assignments. Marcia Linn and Sherry Hsi note that "multiple activity structures"—including online discussions of anonymous and attributed roles—give students more choices. Providing roles and encouraging specialization in

small groups—and a subsequent exchange of roles—can help students appreciate different learning styles and viewpoints. It is important to have "students, who tend otherwise to gravitate toward certain roles in group work, alternate their roles and assignments when working in small groups." Linn and Hsi underscore the importance of continual trial and refinement, so that teachers can identify the groupings and social activities that work best in particular classrooms.[24]

Teacher Bias: Who Has a "Flair" for Computing?

Teachers' assessments of students may correspond to gender clichés about computer competency. One study finds that teachers tend to define computer "interest" in terms of a "flair" for computing, which is in turn equated with the inclination (more often male) to "tinker" with computers. Although in one study male and female students received similarly high marks on exams, teachers attributed girls' success to their diligence and methodical work, whereas even underachieving boys were thought to have an intuitive interest in or "flair" for computers.[25]

Male and female teachers perceive their students' interests in computers somewhat differently. When asked which group of students "is more interested in the 'mechanics' of computer technology," 71 percent of male teachers answer "male students," and only 1 percent answer "female students." More than one-third of male teachers (36 percent) answer that male students "enjoy applied uses and experiences with computers" more than female students do. Female teachers, in contrast, are more likely than male teachers to perceive boys and girls as being "about equal" in their interest in computers. Sixty-six percent of female teachers, for example, find male and female students "about equal" in terms of which group "uses technology more freely and frequently," and 70 percent feel that boys and girls are equal in their enjoyment of "abstract problems" with computers. Female teachers are in agreement with male teachers, however, that female students are more fearful of mistakes on the computers. The interaction of how teachers see students and how students see themselves is obviously a complicated and mutually reinforcing one. But a pattern is clear: Female teachers see girl students as more competent—almost more competent than they see themselves. Male teachers are more likely to describe female students in the passive and disinterested terms with which girls describe themselves in the Foundation's focus group research.[26]

> *Some students have a lot of computer knowledge and others have none. Those that know the computer either monopolize it or end up doing work for those that know little about the computer.*
>
> —teacher survey, on "worst experience" with technology

We face a classroom situation that in many ways seems stuck in time, even as the technology itself races ahead. In the mid 1980s, Turkle found that girls' "computer reticence" stemmed from a perceived conflict between femininity and an interest in computers. There is evidence that this notion persists today. Janet Schofield's research on classroom interaction describes how girls attempt to reconcile traditional feminine ideals with computer accomplishments by minimizing those accomplishments to render them nonthreatening. Girls may downplay their competency and skill by engaging in "feminine" rituals in the classroom such as minimizing their successes, gossiping, grooming, or paying excessive or flirtatious attention to boys. Or they may try to offer advice to boys in ways that they think will not undermine male egos.

Other research observes that girls who behave aggressively in computer-rich settings risk becoming unpopular with boys and girls alike. In this context, a passive response often seems the safest and most rational one.[27]

RECOMMENDATIONS

Design for equity. Evolving an equitable and effective "wired classroom" will require experimentation and diligent attention to the social dynamics of classroom computing. Some guidelines include:

• *Encourage multiple approaches to learning.* Learning with methods such as reciprocal teaching, project-based learning, self-explanation, collaborative learning, computer-based manipulatives, and construction environments can support learning that stands a good chance of including girls and boys with a wide variety of learning styles.

• *Design—and redesign—group work.* Gender needs to be taken into account when students work in groups. Teachers need to experiment with different groupings of students when they set up group work. Teachers need to reward collaborative work and encourage students' roles to alternate as they work together.

• *Provide teachers with written guidelines* for acceptable student behavior and "etiquette" when using information technology, especially the Internet. Have students—and parents—sign contracts on e-culture etiquette and standards. Prepare teachers for "worst moments" when students access inappropriate sites, and equip teachers to have a conversation with students about hate speech, violence, and sex in the cyberculture.

CHAPTER 3

EDUCATIONAL

SOFTWARE AND GAMES:

Rethinking the "Girls' Game"

EDUCATIONAL SOFTWARE AND GAMES

Rethinking the "Girls' Game"

This report considers educational software and computer games together because the line between them has become increasingly blurry. Parents buying games for their children often are hoping that they will have educational content, while educators choosing software for their classrooms are often comparing them to the engaging computer game as a gold standard.[28] Teachers reason that if designers can make computer games so entertaining as to be termed "addictive," why can't some of that talent be used to design educational materials? Furthermore, over the past two decades, generations of children have been socialized into the computer culture through computer games.

From the standpoint of gender equity, however, educators' interests in emulating games is very problematic. The commission noted that most computer games today are designed by men for men. They often have subject matter of interest to boys, or feature styles of interaction known to be comfortable for boys. They are also aggressively marketed to boys. Much educational software targeted for the classroom has similar shortcomings. A review of popular mathematics computer programs intended for grades kindergarten through six showed that only 12 percent of the gender-identifiable characters were female, and that these characters played passive traditional roles, such as "princess." While male and female elementary-age students could name software with male characters, only 6 percent could think of any software with female characters. Another study, reviewing 30 randomly selected software programs used in U.S. schools, found that of the 3,033 characters noted in the graphics and text, only 30 percent were female, and only 4 percent were identified as nonwhite or ethnic. Eighty-one percent of demonstrably "ethnic" characters were male. Women appeared more than men only in the categories of "domestic work" and "manual labor," and 80 percent of all characters featured in "adventure" or "leadership" roles were male. Male characters similarly had a broader range of roles, appearing in 90 separate activities, in comparison to the 55 activities in which female characters appeared. Global and multicultural perspectives in the software focused extensively on themes of war, colonization, aggression, and subjugation.[29]

A great many teachers surveyed for this report seem not to have noticed gender bias in software designed for the classroom. Twenty-one percent of the 900 tech-savvy teachers surveyed by the commission respond that they "don't know" how they would assess software for gender equity, a larger percentage of uncertain responses than for other questions. In response to an open-ended question that asked teachers to "describe the gender differences, if any, they have noted in educational software packages," more than half (58 percent) report that they have not observed any differences in the software, nor have they observed noteworthy gender patterns in use or content. A fair number say, "I haven't really noticed any, but haven't really looked for any, either."

When teachers do note gender bias—as did roughly 40 percent of the respondents to the Foundation's teacher survey—virtually all report that they feel the software caters to male students' interests or learning styles. "Most software 'feels' like it is targeted for boys: action packed, scoring points, winning situations," writes a teacher. "This is not how the teenage female mind works." Another observes, "If it calls for knocking things down or something, the girls perceive it as just for boys and they do not even bother with it. When it comes to communicating and creating writing and pictures, then the girls are way ahead of the boys. But one thing is for certain—when games are available during recess, nine times out of 10, the boys are [playing them]." Some teachers write of software that ascribes to girls what they characterize as "passive," "girly," "fluffy," or simply "traditional" roles. These teachers note that male characters "still get the juicy roles," the lion's share of "adventure" and "logic questions," and a "stronger and more competent" persona in the game. Others observe that girls' competencies and roles are linked to creative projects in software, with "action for boys and artsy stuff for girls."

Change: But in What Direction?

The commission believes that it is possible to have an impact on the game and software culture: The continuing growth of both industries depends on developing more of a relationship with girls. In recent years, the game industry has begun to target girls as a virtually untapped market niche. Analysts now predict that this segment of the computer entertainment market will experience the most dramatic growth of any in the coming years, expanding to more than $400 million in sales in the year 2000.

When the commission discussed possible directions for change in software, it began (as most people do) with Mattel's interactive CDs for girls, the computer games in the Barbie series. The first of these CDs was the Barbie Fashion Designer, in which users can design and fabricate dresses as well as select clothes for a virtual Barbie fashion show. The New York Times reported that "Barbie Fashion Designer sold half a million copies in its first two months—it is not only the biggest girl game on the market but the top-selling children's software title of all time."[30] Many

consider Mattel's Barbie series as the signature "pink software"—software that is designed with girls' traditional interests in mind. Commissioners were divided in their opinions about pink software as an entry point for girls into computing. Some held very negative feelings, pointing out that the software is designed to include girls but it does so in a way that circumscribes their choices, often featuring them in passive, stereotypically "women's roles." Commissioner Yasmin Kafai's research shows that when the software industry uses market research paradigms to open up girls' markets, they create as much as they reflect gender-specific niches and, in the process, circumscribe the imaginations of both boys and girls.[31]

Other commissioners had less critical feelings about pink software. They argued that software has historically been "blue" for boys, "pandering" to male fantasies about violence and aggression. They noted that this software had made boys comfortable with computing: Boys grew into men who felt a sense of ownership of the computer culture. Why deny girls the same kind of access? Given the choice between killing and fashion designing, why criticize the latter? In the end, the commission was persuaded that some girls would develop a comfort with computing through games that are designed with conventionally feminine roles and tasks, but that the future of gender-equitable computing depends on rethinking the question of software. When girls from our focus groups describe the games and software that appeal to them (see "Themes and Content," page 33), they speak about games that allow role playing, identity experiments, and simulations to work through real-life problems. If these were the attributes of pink software, few would object to them for either boys or girls. Indeed, one might well conclude that what would make girls more welcome in the software and game culture would enrich that culture for everyone—boys as well as girls.

Software targeted at a specific gender tends to deal with stereotypes too often. Software for girls tends to be frilly and cutesy, whereas material for boys tends to be tough and masculine. Software should be gender-neutral ... as the real world is to a degree.

—teacher survey, on gender and software

To make play in the digital universe as appealing to girls as it now is to boys—and thereby to provide girls the same opportunities to encounter new technologies in a natural, playful way—digital play spaces have to become more sophisticated. They have to permit flexible decision-making, multiple stories, and perspectives, qualities that are not "girl-specific" so much as they are user-friendly, customizable, personalizable, and inviting to a range of players.

Token Gestures vs. Rethinking Games

It is not enough to make "token gestures" in software—as one teacher surveyed put it, "tossing a token female or black" into science software. As a solution to the problem, some teachers advocate the use of "neuter" characters: "Sometimes packages focus on male characters in their stories," one teacher writes. "But then again, sometimes software companies try to overcompensate because gender equity is such an issue that they make obvious and laughable attempts at creating female 'hero' characters. It's almost worse to try so darn hard. What's wrong with making the main character in these software packages be neuter?" A few other teachers find the effort to make "neuter" characters condescending and unreal. The world, after all, is not comprised of neutered bunnies. A few teachers suggest that since the characters presented in software are, in general, so far from students' experiences and life circumstances, the emphasis should be placed on making software that students are able to

customize rather than trying to develop a set of characters that are appropriate for all.[32]

Differences of opinion over gender-neutral software are indicative of a larger state of confusion concerning software and equity. Parents, teachers, and school administrators shopping for "gender-equitable" software often lack criteria for selection. Even in the very few school districts that have gender equity criteria for the purchase of software, the criteria are fairly static, calling for "balanced representations" of cultural, ethnic, and racial groups. The criteria do not address design issues, play styles, or other less tangible content criteria.[33]

The problem with most gender issues within educational software is that they are gender-neutral. I teach eighth grade. [My students] are at an age when gender is something they are thinking about and confused about. The software should be addressing their needs instead of utilizing non-gendered beings such as animals and other animated creatures. Gender differences are not being given their just due. The students appreciate discussing the differences and negotiating roles. Even math programs can address differences.

—teacher survey, on gender and software

After their review of the literature on software, commissioners agreed that criteria for software selection and courseware evaluation need to go beyond: "Is this software free of violent images?" or "Does this software involve clothes shopping?" Criteria must consider learning styles and students' attitudes toward computers to ensure that software does not appeal narrowly to only one (often male-identified) learning style or set of preferences. And criteria must consider models that empower students to be software "designers," to have greater control of their gaming

> *Most programs are games and have no interaction between students or any other people.*
>

environments. For example, Kafai's research finds that boys adopt more "female" design features in their game designs than vice versa, and demonstrate far more variability in their game preferences than is recognized in commercial models of "boys'" games. Hence, market research-driven paradigms of how to make games have gender appeal do not necessarily capture the range of interests and preferences that boys and girls would bring to games if they were put in the roles of empowered designers.[34]

> *During my first year of teaching I taught a fourth-through-sixth-grade GATE class. After months of waiting, we finally received four computers for our classroom. My students strutted in and loudly exclaimed, "Show us the games! We've mastered them all." Since I've had a lot of training in multimedia and other aspects in technology education, I looked at them and said, "No, no, in this class we don't PLAY the games, we MAKE the games." Seeing all 31 pairs of eyes light up at that comment and become truly hooked in technology has been one of my favorite memories in seven years of teaching.*
>

General Design Features

The girls who participated in focus groups for the Foundation's research were asked to design their ideal computer game for girls (software, online, or video) and to discuss their preferences among existing game options. For the most part, the girls describe characteristics that converge with some qualities that boys value in games, and challenge the notion that software should be designed and marketed to girls and boys as distinct market "niches." Appealing characteristics include:

• Rich narrative and intricate, multi-level games. (Says a Richmond middle school student, "Make it a game where you have different options—each way you go there are different passages that lead you somewhere else.")

• Engaging characters (preferably female or non-gendered, personalizable, and customizable).

• Ample opportunities for communication and collaboration.

• Roles involving positive social action (such as guiding characters through a set of puzzles or challenges).

• Challenge at the appropriate level of difficulty.

• Social interaction both on-screen and between players—opportunities to build new relationships.

• Opportunities to design or create. (One high school girl describes it this way: "Trivial Pursuit meets Tetris meets paintbrush.")

• Strategy and skill requirements. (Says one respondent, "I like games that actually have like a strategy, not just shooting a gun at people.")[35]

Themes and Content

The girls in these focus groups say that they prefer games where they make things rather than destroy things. Many girls talk about computer games where they get to simulate real life, invent characters and personalities, or play with worldviews and identity on

The game would probably star a teenage girl. She would have to go through different challenges like choosing not to smoke, or real-life questions like that. It would help people not to ruin their lives and help people who might be having family problems, like parents who are getting divorced.

—Washington, DC, middle school student

the screen. A Fairfax high school student imagines games where you "pick out a character, choose music, pick out a personality (job, hair, complexion), live [as the] person for a year, make their decisions, design a living space; [you] must give time to study for tests, must get an A at the end of the year to beat the game." She continues: "There would be a choice of being female or male. Then they would start in the morning and choose what they want to do that day. When they start the day, they would be faced with different situations, and, depending on how they choose to get out of the situation, it will become easier or harder." A middle school girl from Washington, DC, would design "a video game for girls, telling the computer how your life has been and how you want it to be in the future, like a doll kind of thing." Other girls imagine more extensive identity games that entail the creation of personae and the building of worlds.[36]

Many girls advocate games that simulate "realistic" adolescent experiences. Girls in the focus groups

describe games in which characters must navigate the dangers and choices that are part of girls' lives—and of their lives. For example, one high school student from Baltimore says that her ideal games are closely related to everyday life: "My game would incorporate creativity, and it would be realistic, because I hate video games that are so fake." Girls elaborate these "real games" as ones where they can play out different life choices, especially those linked to gender roles and identity. Girls in these groups describe games that are the psychological and social extensions of popular girl software that involves cosmetic and wardrobe makeover and transformation. "The game would be based on real life, the action being in how you react in some situations," one middle school girl summarizes. Another high school girl imagines a game that shows different stages of growing up "so you learn from your mistakes and you can choose your own path. This way it can relate to everyone."

My game would be a game where you could describe your own image of a world that you would like it to be. Like you could design buildings, houses, whatever you would want the world to be.

—Baltimore high school student

A Richmond middle schooler writes a detailed account of a game with realistic scenarios and a moral message:

My game would be about a little girl in distress being saved and taken to freedom. The main figure would be a teenage girl between the ages of 16 and 18. The purpose would be to show girls how to overcome problems and fears. It would start with a girl facing boy problems with her parents at home, and lots of peer pressure. Different questions would come about and her answer to the questions would determine her outcome. During the game, different figures would appear, such as a teacher, a minister, and a friend. They would try to help her make a good choice or a bad choice, but the choice would be hers. At the end, if all the right choices were made, she would be greatly rewarded with her greatest desire.

> *Have a main character [a girl] who has missions to break stereotypes. For example, she would play baseball and win, and prove everyone wrong, or play a rock concert.*
>
> —Baltimore high school student

Other girls who describe games based on real adolescent experiences see the game as a "mentor," a proxy for parents or friends, perhaps, who could provide advice on topics that adults may not want to discuss. Realistic scenario games were particularly popular among two focus groups held with Hispanic and African American students. Some commissioners thought this may indicate a need for mentoring and positive images of problem solving. One student specifically describes a computer mentor— "someone or something that really does give you advice when you're going through a bad situation whether you're

> *[I want] something intellectual, fun, stimulating—[something that would] have tricky secrets that make you stop to think. The main figure, I don't really know, it wouldn't have to be a person—it could even consist of questions or pictures. The purpose would be to excel to higher levels nonstop. I would like it to take forever to win the game so it won't get boring.*
>
> —Washington, DC, middle school student

in school or anywhere. Also something that some parents don't want to discuss is sex, drugs, etc., and when your parents are divorced, a girl needs help on certain periods of her life to have your second parents."

By itself, becoming engaged in game-playing does not constitute technological fluency, but game and software cultures have been important factors in making boys and men feel comfortable with computing, and this path needs to be opened to girls and boys who have not found the style and themes of existing software appealing.

Nontraditional Software

Girls in many cases describe software characteristics that researchers have also found appealing to a wide variety of students, including those who are not "traditional" computer users. For example, in a study of third graders (ages eight to nine) in an urban elementary school, Anne L. Davidson and Janet W. Schofield observed the creation of a positive technology environment when one teacher offered children opportunities to use computers to develop relationships. The teacher used software that enabled children to build a virtual community. The particular software, known as MOO (short for multiple user, object-oriented) was used to engage children in reading and enhance their writing skills. The virtual environment contained storytellers, and the children could take on the roles of characters and have conversations with other users.[37]

> *The point would be to see what you would do in everyday situations, situations you may be faced with growing up.*
>
> —Richmond middle school student

Overall, Davidson and Schofield observed that girls who participated in this class showed decreased technical anxiety and increased technical confidence by the end of the course. Furthermore, girls developed new technical skills in the innovative MOO setting. Several features contributed to the teacher's success in creating an interesting and broadly appealing and equitable learning context: The teacher utilized an online environment that was not laden with traditionally masculine themes such as conquest. Instead, the online environment conveyed an inviting place for all students to communicate with others; the teacher played an active role in organizing students' work collaboratively. Students were assigned to work in pairs and the teacher rotated to different groups as they needed help. Collaboration eventually became the ethos of the whole class. Finally, the activities engaged girls' interests. They appreciated the ability to learn about online characters and to develop relationships online and off-line.

[I envision] students at computers, working on examples set up by teachers during lessons. The teacher could see who is understanding and who is not. Those who understand could move on, and those who need more instruction would receive it.

—teacher survey, on the future of the classroom

Another promising study explored games with gender-neutral themes and characters. Andee Rubin and her colleagues at TERC studied boys and girls using the CD-ROM "Logical Journey of the Zoombinis," a program designed to teach mathematics, logic, and set theory to eight-to-12-year-olds (third- to fifth-graders). The researchers found that while there were many individual differences in the ways students played the game, there was not a significant difference along gender lines. Software that engages both boys and girls, they conclude, tends to permit varied levels of collaboration, offer rich problems with multiple solutions, and provide a coherent, nonviolent narrative. Rubin writes that both boys and girls responded favorably to a "sense of conflict and potential resolution: The characters are in jeopardy and the player's actions can help them."[38]

Given the diverse ability levels of students and the emphasis on designing lessons appropriate for the individual student, I believe that computers and technology offer the best way to provide this. ... Ironically, it seems that computers and technology will be the way to provide more personalized instruction tailored to individual interests and needs.

—teacher survey, on the future of the classroom

Sherry Hsi experimented with a tool to facilitate online discussions, investigating how students respond to anonymous and identified communication. Hsi found that students, especially female students, were more willing to participate when they could choose to remain anonymous than when all comments were attributed. She found that although the quality of contributions was similar for attributed and anonymous material, students had individual preferences for a particular format of discussion. In interviews, males and females both commented on the stereotyping that can occur in attributed electronic classroom discussions. Students believe that peer-anonymous discussions could open the discussion to more students. Students have the opportunity to get feedback on views that they fear might be ridiculed or misinterpreted by their peers in a face-to-face context. Adolescents are insecure and acutely worried about peer reception of their ideas. Women and minority students fear that their contributions, particularly about mathematics and science, might be received with prejudice. The opportunity to make anonymous comments in peer discussion allows these students to voice their own ideas without attracting potentially stereotyping responses.[39]

Finally, researcher Schofield analyzed the use of geometry computer "tutor" in several classrooms, and found that it allowed teachers to dispense more individualized attention and advice to their students. Further, it encouraged self-paced learning for slower and faster students, and introduced controls against students "skipping over" concepts in the curriculum that they did not truly understand. In partnership, rather than as substitutes for one another, the computer tutor and the teacher promoted more effective classroom techniques and individualized learning in unanticipated ways.[40]

RECOMMENDATIONS

Focus on girls as designers. Educators, parents, and others should help girls imagine themselves early in life as designers and producers of software and games, rather than as consumers or end users of games. Girls need opportunities at an early age to express their technological imaginations in a variety of media. Supporting activities that encourage girls to think further about the social history, purpose, function, and form of devices they see around them and envision for the future enable girls to become more attuned to observing, analyzing, and contributing to the built environment. This kind of activity paves the way for future hands-on technological design.

Rethink what constitutes a "girls' game"—and a "boys' game." The computer game industry, educators, parents, software designers, and marketers do not need to label software specifically as "girls' games" or "boys' games"; instead, software for both classroom and home settings should focus on the many design elements that engage the interests of a broad range of learners, including both boys and girls, among them "nontraditional" computer users who do not identify with the "nerd" or "hacker" stereotypes.

The following 10 design characteristics are conducive to engaging a broader array of learners, boys and girls, with computer environments:

1. software that is personalizable and customizable. This type of software allows students to create their own characters, scenarios, and endings, and allows them to work independently or collaboratively.

2. games with challenge

3. games involving more strategy and skill

4. games with many levels, intricacies, and complexities

5. flexibility to support multiple narratives

6. constructionist design—one that allows students to create their own objects through the software

7. designs that support collaborative or group work, and encourage social interaction

8. coherent, nonviolent narratives

9. "puzzle connections," such as rich mysteries with multiple resolutions

10. goal-focused rather than open-ended games

The following four content features have been found to be "girl friendly":

1. "identity games" that enable girls to experiment with characters and real-life scenarios. Some of these games enable girls to invent online personalities, identities, and worlds. Some of these games enable girls to experiment with choices about peer pressure, smoking, sexual relationships, etc., and "play out" the consequences of their action.

2. software that has realistic as well as fantastical content; games that function as simulations of authentic contexts and situations

3. software structured around a conflict with potential resolution

4. games that have themes of mystery and adventure

Create a "Caldecott" award for software. Consumers—children, parents, educators, and school districts—need a "seal of approval" that denotes excellence in games just as the American Library Association's Caldecott Medal recognizes excellence in picture books. The software "Caldecott" should reward games that are both "good" in that they engage the user's interest, and "equitable" in that they appeal to a variety of users. The American Association for the Advancement of Science is suggesting a similar strategy for books and films in science.

CHAPTER 4

THE COMPUTER SCIENCE

CLASSROOM:

Call It "Oceanography"

and They Will Come

THE COMPUTER SCIENCE CLASSROOM

Call It "Oceanography" and They Will Come

In the history of computing, women took a pioneering role. They were among the first programmers, as the "ENAIC girls" in World War II, and were amply represented on college campuses when computer science emerged as a discipline in the 1970s. But women's share of computer science bachelor's degrees has declined over time, from a peak of 37 percent in 1984 to 28 percent in 1995. In high school, girls are less likely than boys to enroll in computer science classes, and this disparity increases with more advanced classes. Overall, girls account for fewer than 17 percent of those taking the Advanced Placement Computer Science exam. When girls do take computer classes at the high school and community college level, they are significantly more likely than boys to enroll in clerical and data-entry classes. (See "Computer Science AP Test-Taking, by Sex, Race, and Ethnicity" on page 42.)[41]

According to a 1997 survey of 652 college-bound high school students in Silicon Valley, Boston, and Austin, Texas, for the Garnett Foundation, 50 percent of both males and females feel that the discipline of computer science is "geared toward men." The stereotype of computer science is both masculine and negative. When asked, girls and women describe a prevailing concern that computer science will stunt their diverse range of intellectual pursuits and interests, and that it involves work that is tedious, sedentary, and—most critically—antisocial.[42] Additionally, many students complain that current courses in computer science are frustrating and poorly taught, or that they are structured to weed students out rather than to encourage students to come into the field. To attract a more diverse set of students, these courses need to be made more accessible, and more connected to topics beyond engineering.[43]

A "Pipeline" or a "Web"?

Several commissioners confirm girls' reservations about computer science, noting that computing classes are often bastions of poor pedagogy. Commissioner Mae Jemison stresses that it would not be a desirable outcome simply to groom more young women to be computer programmers if that discipline is taught in a way that does not foster the growth of important analytical and scientific skills. The commission acknowledges the central importance of computer science as a prerequisite to a variety of disciplines, but notes that in the next few decades, the field is likely to become an integral part of several disciplines, ranging from architecture to the life sciences and medicine. Thus, there are likely to be multiple paths to competence, aside from the attainment of a degree with a formal computer science major. In this respect, computer science differs from other disciplines such as biology or chemistry characterized by a "pipeline" or linear, progressive path to expertise. The involvement of computer science skills in many disciplinary fields makes it both more imperative that a broader range of students achieve some fluency with it, as well as more likely that they will encounter it in school through nontechnological subject areas. The commission recommended an alternative metaphor to the pipeline—the "web" or the "net"—to denote the multiple entry points for girls and women into expertise with computer science and technology. (See "Girls' and Boys' Computer-Related Course-Taking, K-12" on page 45.)

Computer Science AP Test-Taking, by Sex, Race, and Ethnicity

The Advanced Placement test in computer science is a three-hour examination pegged to college-level course material covered in AP high school classes. Students who score a 3 or above are eligible to receive college credit for their work, although many schools require a higher score of 4 or 5 to earn college credit.

There are two computer science AP exam options. The Computer Science "A" exam covers topics in a first-semester introductory college course in computer science, while the Computer Science "AB" exam covers topics in a full-year introductory college course.

Differences in Numbers of Test-Takers

Data from 1999 reveal that 11,793 students total took the Computer Science "A" exam. Of these students, 9,834, or 83 percent, were men; 1,959, or 17 percent, were women. On the more extensive, more difficult Computer Science "AB" examination, women comprised 9 percent (611) of the 6,450 total test-takers. Men comprised the vast majority of test-takers, at 91 percent.

Differences in Scores

Not only do far fewer women take the computer science AP exams: Those young women who do less frequently score a credit-eligible grade of 3, 4, or 5. Forty-one percent of female test-takers scored the lowest grade of 1, compared to 28 percent of the male test-takers. Roughly the same percentage of males and females scored a credit-ineligible grade of 2, yet smaller percentages of female test-takers scored grades of 3 (17 percent of women; 19 percent of men), 4 (20 percent of women; 25 percent of men),

or the highest grade of 5 (10 percent of women; 17 percent of men).

Racial/Ethnic and Gender Differences in Numbers and Scores

Racial and ethnic differences in test-taking rates are evident among the populations of both male and female test-takers. Of all the test-takers who stated their race/ethnicity, 65 percent were white, 22 percent Asian American, 5 percent African American, 5 percent Hispanic, and 3 percent "other."

Relative to their representation in the U.S. population (1.6 percent of U.S. residents), Asian American women were robustly represented as computer science AP test-takers, at 28 percent of the women overall. Aside from a lower percentage of 1 scorers

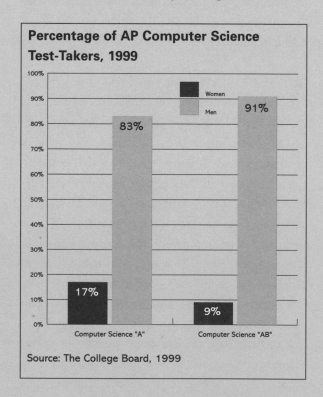

Percentage of AP Computer Science Test-Takers, 1999

■ Women
□ Men

Computer Science "A": Women 17%, Men 83%
Computer Science "AB": Women 9%, Men 91%

Source: The College Board, 1999

(36 percent), Asian American women's scores mirrored the averages for women overall.

African American women took the AP exam at a higher rate than African American men. African American women constituted 10 percent of the women taking the exam, whereas African American men constituted 3 percent of the men taking the exam. However, 83 percent of African American women scored 1 on the exam, more than twice the percentage for all women with this score (41 percent). A similar pattern is evident for African American men who took the exam.

Perhaps most striking among female and male test-takers are the disturbingly low numbers of Hispanics who take the exam. Only 127 Hispanic girls in the country took the "A" exam, and only 16 took the "AB" exam. No Puerto Ricans took the "AB" exam, and only 12 took the "A" exam. Researcher Jane Margolis similarly notes that only seven Hispanic girls took the computer science AP exam in California in 1999, despite their sizeable representation in the California population overall. According to the 1990 census, Hispanic girls ages 15 to 19 comprise 9 percent of the state population.

Furthermore, a higher percentage of Hispanic females (63 percent) scored 1 on the exam than did female test-takers overall (41 percent.) A similar pattern is evident for Hispanic males who took the exam.

The metaphor of the web or the net denotes that computing should be encountered across the curriculum, and also suggests some changes in the way computer science courses should be taught. Courses in computer science would do well to put students in a position where they are using technology to design and build, an approach that is not only engaging, but enables students to appropriate information technology—to make it their own by applying it to problems and areas of interest to them. This constructionist framework leaves open the possibility for students to approach course material with different intellectual styles, and for different reasons and interests. Computer science instruction that emphasizes the "web" of associations between programming, design, and other areas of the curriculum would help to attract a more diverse group of learners, and would advance computer fluency for all students.

Additionally, computer science courses would do well to discuss the interplay between computers and people in real-life situations, an aspect of the computer culture that girls say they value. Studies have shown that when teachers have tried to demonstrate how programming applied to real life, their classroom examples gravitated toward sports statistics, even when the programming task at hand was open-ended.[44]

Institutional, Logistical, and Social Issues

There are significant opportunities for changing the computer science curriculum. In most school settings, the computer science curriculum is not fixed or determined by national curricular standards. But there are significant obstacles to change as well: In particular, the Advanced Placement Computer Science exam shapes the computing curriculum and becomes a "driver" of its emphasis and tone.

Some commissioners feel that girls would be more drawn to computer science courses if they were not located in the mathematics department, that this placement burdened girls' relationship to computing with their complex and often conflicted involvement with mathematics.[45] Others disagree, pointing out that women are equally represented in mathematics courses in high school today, and that it would be worse for these classes to be in the science department. The best strategy would be the creation of "technology" departments that could develop an expertise for helping teachers infuse computing throughout the curriculum.

Other logistical changes include scheduling computer science classes to minimize scheduling conflicts with classes popular with girls, and increasing the number of electives students can choose, since computer science courses are rarely girls' elective of first choice.[46]

Received wisdom among college students is that introductory first-year computer science classes are "killers" designed to weed out students rather than to invite participation. Research suggests that female students tend to evolve an interest in computer science over time and so the competitive nature of the first-year "triage" class may needlessly weed out students. The same perceptions and misgivings may exist at the high school level. (See "Computer Science and Technology Course-Taking in One School District" on page 46.)[47]

Additionally, research finds that girls work in the area of computer science with several social factors against them. First, because girls are usually outnumbered in computer science classes, they are at risk of social isolation, which makes learning more difficult.[48] Second, girls may worry that doing well in computer science will raise questions or anxieties about their femininity or gender identity, an issue that has been stubbornly resistant to the information technology "revolution"

of the past decades. In the mid-1980s, Turkle reported that in her studies of computer science classes, women turned away from computing because they felt they could not reconcile it with their sense of being feminine. Nearly two decades later, Schofield's observations of computer science classes show similar patterns.[49] Schofield notes that boys repeatedly referred to girls' femininity and appearance when interacting with girls in computer science classes, distracting girls from their work. Third, it is not unusual for girls and minorities who enroll in computer science classes to come to these classes with fewer skills than their white male counterparts. Many of the white males have a great deal of exposure to computers at home, and bring these skills to class with them. But the teachers Schofield observed did not acknowledge or address these prior inequities. Doing so would be helpful. When such disparity in experience goes unacknowledged, it is more likely that less experienced students will feel they are not good enough to do the work, although the disparity depends on history, not talent.[50]

RECOMMENDATIONS

Redesign computer science courses for equity—and better instruction. As presently taught, the computer science curriculum may dissuade participation—not only from girls, but also from learners who are not enamored of programming or technology for its own sake. Girls and young women who have described their experiences with computer science point to specific recommendations for refining the design of these classes to make them more equitable and engaging to a broader array of learners. They include the following:

Integrate computer science through the curriculum. Have computer science go beyond program-

Girls' and Boys' Computer-Related Course-Taking, K-12

Fewer boys and girls are enrolling in computer science classes that prepare students for careers in computer programming and theory. The enrollment drop is puzzling in light of industry needs for technically skilled workers. However, the demand for technical support, coupled with rapid change in technology, may prompt students to opt for certification programs within the high school or informal, ongoing self-education. Cisco, for example, currently sponsors hundreds of "networking academies" in U.S. high schools, through which students may earn certification for particular information technology (IT) jobs. Novell and Microsoft also offer certification programs in school. Reports of students who earn competitive salaries for IT work and web design services even before high school graduation may further minimize the appeal of high school or college programs in computer science.

Computer applications courses in graphic arts and computer-aided design, not especially common in high school, attract very few girls. One-semester computer science courses attract significantly more males than females; a similar, though less dramatic, pattern appears in two-semester courses. Girls, however, are significantly more likely than boys to enroll in clerical and data-entry classes, the 1990s version of typing.

Percentage of 1990 and 1994 High School Graduates Taking Computer Courses, by Sex

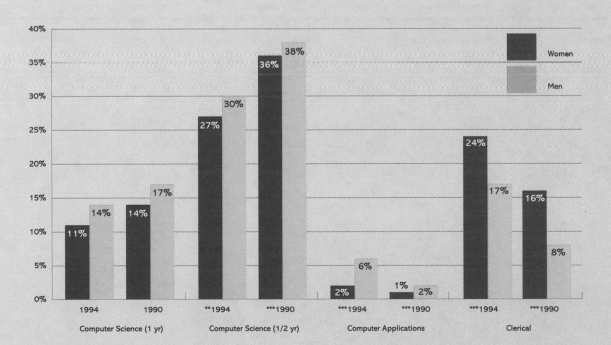

** Significant at p<.05
*** Significant at p<.01

Source: U.S. Department of Education, National Center for Education Statistics, *Vocational Course Taking and Achievement: An Analysis of High School Transcripts and 1990 NAEP Assessment Scores (Washington, DC: 1995)*

Computer Science and Technology Course-Taking in One School District

The Fairfax County Public School District in Fairfax County, Virginia, enrolls 155,993 students and is the 12th-largest public school district in the country. The district boasts a technology-rich learning environment. All classrooms are wired for Internet connection. In 1999 the Fairfax County Human Relations Advisory Committee issued a report on gender equity issues that reviewed district data on course enrollment in math, science, technology, and computer sciences for all high schools in the district.

Noting the persistence of "near-total gender segregation" across the vocational education classes, the report presents data on enrollment in technology-related business education and technical education courses, by sex, race, and ethnicity. As shown on the bar graph below, nearly all (94 percent) of the students in "artificial intelligence" classes were male, as were a large majority (77 percent) of the students in business-computer programming classes. Information systems and desktop publishing classes are less skewed, with 54 percent male and 46 percent female enrollment, respectively. The only class where males do not predominate is word processing, which is consistent with national data. Females comprise 55 percent of the word processing students.

Enrollment in Fairfax County Public School Technology Courses, by Sex, 1998

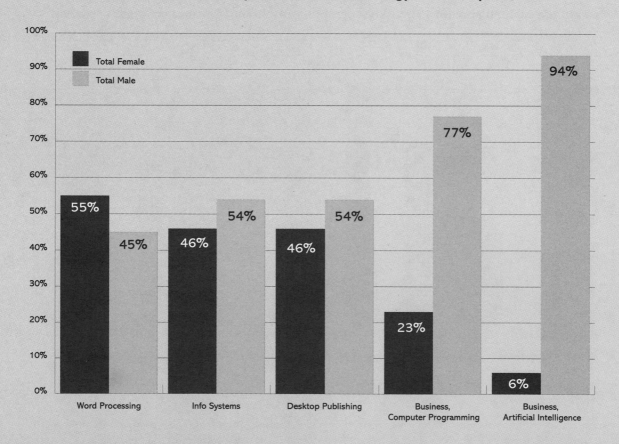

Source: Fairfax County Public Schools

African American and Asian American females enroll in word processing classes at twice the rate of their representation in the high school district population overall. (African Americans are 5 percent of the school population, and 12 percent of word processing students; Asian Americans are 7 percent of the district population, and 14 percent of word processing students.) Caucasian males, in contrast, enroll in "artificial intelligence" classes at twice the rate of their representation in the school population (32 percent of the population and 62 percent of "artificial intelligence" students).

Starker sex differences appear in enrollments in technical education classes, such as technical drawing, architectural drawing, engineering drawing, and electronics. Girls comprise 1 percent of the electronics students, 15 percent of the technical drawing students, and 18 percent of the architectural drawing students.

The Fairfax County report places these figures within the broader context of electives available in district high schools, in order to learn which classes girls take instead of computer science or technical electives. The smallest gender disparities in electives appear in several foreign language courses, chemistry, economics, several history courses, and a few art and music electives. The most dramatic gender disparities—classes where girls outnumber boys, and vice versa, by 30 percent or more—appear in computer architecture, engineering, auto mechanics, network administration, design and technology, micro-electronics, carpentry, computer technology and electronics, and engineering. Girls outnumber boys by 30 percent or more in child care, nursing, dance, cosmetology, fashion marketing, dental careers, food occupations, and animal science.

ming to emphasize how computer science (including programming) is used to solve real-life problems.

• **Teach "tinkering" activities.** Promote exploration of the machines, especially for girls in middle school. Create social environments that will make it more likely that girls will "get under the hood." Promote the possibilities for learners to make the computer their own, in their own way—an approach consistent with a constructionist methodology.

• **Strive for a critical mass of girls in classes.** This may require direct recruiting efforts, or working directly with guidance counselors. It may also require rethinking the prerequisites to computer science courses (such as advanced mathematics) if they are serving as barriers to girls but are really not necessary for success in the course.

• **Design the introductory class as a "pump," not a "filter."** Classes that are designed to filter out students rather than invite them into the discipline may estrange students who otherwise would excel in the field, but who lack the same level of background as other students.

CHAPTER 5

THE SCHOOL IN CONTEXT:
Home, Community, and Work

THE SCHOOL IN CONTEXT
Home, Community, and Work

Trends in home and community use of computer technology raise important questions about the economic and other implications of girls' and women's experience. These larger themes deserve mention, particularly insofar as they interact with school experiences, although a thorough examination is beyond the scope of this report.

Gender equity in the emerging e-culture is one component of larger social equity concerns about unequal technological access and use. Several studies since 1990 have asked whether the infusion of computer technology has diminished or exacerbated existing social inequality. A few recent studies point to a wider access gap in communities and homes than schools. The U.S. Department of Commerce describes a "striking" racial divide for PC ownership: White households are still more than twice as likely to own a computer than black or Hispanic households, a profound gap evident even at household income levels above $75,000. Rates of online access were three times as high for white households as for black or Hispanic households. Education affects the household "penetration rate" as much as income: Thirty-eight percent of those with a college degree have online access, compared with only 9 percent of those with a high school diploma. The report diagnoses a "widening" of the "digital divide" in home use from 1994 to 1997. [51]

The Kaiser Family Foundation released a report in November 1999 that examines children and media, including computer technology. Virtually all children report having a television at home (99 percent); 69 percent report having a computer at home. Kaiser reports that "in a possible indication of things to come, most kids say they prefer computer to TV, if they're forced to choose." Echoing the Department of Commerce findings, this report finds that differences by income are more dramatic in home use than in school use. Children from lower-income neighborhoods are just as likely as those from higher-income communities to have used a computer in school (32 percent to 30 percent) the day before the survey; however, children who live in or go to school in lower-income neighborhoods are much less likely to have a computer anywhere in the home. About half of children in lower-income communities have a computer in the home, with 23 percent reporting Internet access, in contrast to 81 percent of children in higher-income neighborhoods, with 58 percent reporting Internet access. These data underscore the important role of schools and community learning centers in helping to equalize disparities in home computer use and access across income levels. [52]

The Kaiser Family Foundation report found gender differences in media exposure primarily—almost exclusively—around use of computer games, with boys more likely to play computer games than girls. Girls may have fewer informal computing experiences than boys in part because of the disparity in games available that build on their interests. The Department of Commerce identifies female-headed households as among the "least connected" in the country. Studies indicate that women's lower socio-economic standing generally carries over to their ownership of computers. It is probable that the gender gap in home ownership of web-capable machines is linked to women's purchase of second-hand computers, or "inheriting" cast-off computers from acquaintances, partners, or parents.[53]

I envision the classroom of the future with more computers, and more students owning computers at home so they come in with more understanding.

—teacher survey, on the future of the classroom

Other research concludes that parents of boys are more likely to buy computers for them, place them in the boys' rooms, or enroll them in computer camps than parents of girls. As a result, boys tend to come to school with more technology experience.[54]

Although students have access to computers while at school, many students do not have computers at home. Until there's a computer in every house and more programs are cross- or multi-platform, I don't see computers/ technology being the primary resource.

—teacher survey, on the future of the classroom

Almost all teens feel they are better at computers than their parents, and the gulf is especially great between daughters and their mothers. Girls report that their fathers are more comfortable with computer technology than their mothers, and parental examples often reinforce gender stereotypes. Girls commonly report that their dads use computers for very different tasks than their moms, or imagine that their dads have a ubiquitous knowledge of "everything" on the computer, while their mothers have more limited (word processing) skills. "My dad knows everything there is to know, but I had to teach my mom how to turn it on," reports a Fairfax teenager. A girl from Baltimore says that her "dad knows everything about computers and my mom doesn't. So it is mainly my dad."

Another notes, "My mom does use a computer because she was a secretary for so many years; she could do WordPerfect, but when she gets on the Internet, she gets really upset and I try to help her with it and tell her how to do it. She just does not understand what's going on."

My dad is pretty good at the computer. He likes using the computer. He took computer classes and he knows a lot and when I have trouble, I ask him and he'll help me, but my mom, she's not really into computers.

—Fairfax, Virginia, high school student

RECOMMENDATIONS

Introduce girls to technology early to discourage the development of gender stereotypes at home.

Strive for a "family" computer. Among other things, place computers in accessible spaces—not, for example, in a male child's room, or an office. Think about shared or family-centered activities on the computer, rather than viewing computer use as an individual, solitary activity.

Create school-home-community links and partnerships. Introducing schools as community "learning centers" after hours can expand computer access to female-headed and low-income families, presently among the least connected in the country.

Develop intergenerational learning activities. Information technology provides a unique opportunity for daughters and mothers to learn together and to alternate the roles of "expert" and "novice."

COMPUTER CLUBS AND EXTRACURRICULAR ACTIVITIES IN SCHOOLS

In many K-12 schools, the computer lab or club is the place where the most intensive, playful, and unstructured learning happens for students. Labs and clubs, commonly open during lunch hour and after school, can provide more time for learning than formal classes. Yet these voluntary spaces, so crucial to giving students without home access time on the computers, tend to exaggerate gender and racial differences more than classrooms.[55] Schofield, studying lunchtime computer labs, described how they became "bright, white boys' lunch clubs." The lunchtime computer labs became masculine preserves where boys established a culture of competition and bravado based on game play. Girls did not become part of the lunchtime culture. More recently, after-school and "clubhouse" settings are finding ways to break these patterns. Even simple steps such as ensuring students can sign up for time can make a big difference. (See "The Lilith Computer Club" on page 54.)[56]

To ensure equitable participation in such environments, educators and administrators need to avoid social arrangements and educational practices that isolate girls who want to use computers or that allow one group of students to so dominate the setting that others find working there awkward or unwelcoming. Additionally, educators need to compensate for the disparity between boys and girls, rich and poor, and heavy to little prior experience with technology, when establishing clubs and extracurricular activities.

RECOMMENDATIONS

Reconfigure informal spaces. Free spaces for computer use can easily become the tacit property of a small group of students, typically white males. All students should feel welcome in these spaces.

Infuse computing into a range of clubs. Community groups, administrators, and educators should consider establishing clubs and activities that use technology in the service of other interests, for example, a design club.

Consider single-sex after-school and extracurricular opportunities for girls to socialize and work on computer-related projects together.

Start early. Existing science and technology after-school programs and summer camps tend to reach out to girls in high school. These activities are important, but they may come too late. Girls seem to form beliefs about their relationships with technology when they are quite young.[57]

The Lilith Computer Club
by Susannah Camric

Part I - Spring 1997

Walk into my high school computer lab on any regular school day, and you will immediately notice the wide range of computer technology available for student use. You might also notice the ease with which students in the lab manipulate the computers and access their programs. Look a little more closely, however, and you will see that the overwhelming majority of these students are boys. On a typical afternoon in the lab, for example, there were 40 boys—and me. This is the way things have been for years—and that this is the way they could easily remain.

In my middle school computer lab, the teacher was famous for outbursts at students who made mistakes and caused difficulties in the computer network. As a result, whenever I sat down at a computer next to a girl who was a beginning computer user and suggested that we experiment with a new command or program, her response was always: "Let's not do it. I don't want to screw anything up." Yet successful computer students claim that in order to succeed with computers, you must be willing to experiment.

Software. In my middle school, there were three favorite computer games:

• "Spectre VR," which involved a futuristic-looking vehicle attempting to annihilate other vehicles with bombs

• a typing program based on rockets and bombs

• another game (name unknown, since a large cluster of boys chased me away every time I approached it) which involved soldier-style figures running around killing enemies

Only two games were not based on violence: "Tetris," which boys at my school had organized into a competitive sport with elaborate tournaments that intimidated beginning girls; and "Disney's Coaster," a happy-sounding roller coaster designing game. But even this game was distressing; it required you to design a roller coaster for a panel of "riders," who gave nearly every design a bitingly cynical review. To top it off, all the "riders" were male, except for a repulsive-looking elderly woman and a "dumb blond," in a low-cut top and makeup, who compared roller coasters to kissing her boyfriends. The boys in my class found these characters and their critical barbs humorous, but the girls seemed to find them discouraging—and this was our best software choice.

Atmosphere of School Computer Labs. In middle and high school, I have often been the one girl in a computer lab with 30 to 40 boys. In middle school, I was often told simply to go away by boys who had logged into illegal sites and thought I might tell the teacher what they were up to. … Occasionally, I would gather a few friends and we would go to the computer club, an after-school activity with nearly 50 participants, all (except for us) male. There, we would watch politely as the boys demonstrated the new software that the school had obtained. Sometimes there was a chance to "chat" on America Online, but the boys would refuse to let us near the keyboard, and we could only look on as they typed in sexual remarks and jokes.

Part II - Summer 1999

After writing the first part of this paper in early 1997, I set to work on a proposal to create girl-targeted weekly computer clubs and an annual girls' computer conference. I sent the paper to a variety of individuals whom I thought might be interested in working with me in developing and implementing the program. Several expressed an interest in working further on the issues, and after what seemed like hundreds of phone calls, we came together to form the steering committee of a nonprofit organization that came to be called the Lilith Computer Group.

The organization's first task was to establish girl-targeted computer clubs in four of Madison's middle schools. The four schools serve populations that are very diverse, both economically and ethnically. Each club is led by a volunteer "club leader"—a position that has been filled by both middle school teachers interested in computers and by local computer professionals. Often the leaders are assisted by other volunteers, who may be parents, local computer professionals, or students from the University of Wisconsin. Typically, clubs meet after school once or twice a week for hour-long sessions, which are attended by 20-25 girls. At these sessions, girls are given the opportunity to learn computer skills in supportive, "fun," and nonthreatening environments.

During the Lilith Computer Group's first year, club leaders set their own curricula. In the group's second year, however, a grant from the American Association of University Women Educational Foundation enabled a committee of Madison teachers and steering committee members to … develop a curriculum guide which included a set of lesson plans. …

The second task of the Lilith Computer Group has been to plan, organize, and host an annual "Lilith Computer Fair." The first was held in May 1998 at the University of Wisconsin-Madison School of Engineering. The second was held there in April 1999. Attended by roughly 60 girls from the four Lilith after-school clubs (plus a few interested boys), the Lilith Computer Fair introduced participants to computers in a wide variety of settings, and allowed attendees to observe university personnel in their work with computers and to experience advanced technology for themselves in hands-on laboratory settings. Both fairs opened with a panel of women in various careers in which computers are used on a daily basis (panel members have included a veterinarian, a weaver, an interior decorator, an engineer, and a security officer). Girls then proceeded to hands-on sessions that focused on Internet exploration, Adobe Photo Shop, and a variety of other applications. After these sessions, attendees visited sites on the University of Wisconsin campus where computers are used in unusual ways. These have included a virtual reality engineering lab, a dance studio, a department of textile design, a biotechnology center, and a meteorology lab.

The Lilith Computer Group has thus far met with great success. Its programs have enabled a diverse set of middle school girls to develop competence and confidence in technology use. One area where these activities have met with particularly notable success is in attracting girls who do not have home access to computers: Often such students—many of them students of color—are not otherwise involved in school extracurricular activities. Club leaders have observed that the Lilith Computer Group program serves as a positive influence in these girls' lives beyond teaching about computers.

THE WORK ENVIRONMENT

Several news articles and reports have sounded an alarm that the United States faces a shortage of skilled workers in information technology and computer science, and changes in immigration law have been proposed as one solution to the shortfall. Estimates are that by 2010, one in every four new jobs will be "technically oriented"—involve the use, design, application, or maintenance of computers. The Information Technology Association of America reports that 71 percent of large and mid-size information technology companies believe demand exceeds skilled workers, and one information technology position is vacant for every 10 information technology employees in the same company.[58]

The overall alarm about an anemic information technology work force, for example, is less surprising when considered in light of sex segregation on the labor market. Women comprise roughly 20 percent of information technology professionals. (See "Women in Information Technology Careers" on page 57.) Women receive less than 20 percent of bachelor's degrees in computer science and engineering-related technology. The relative disinterest in technology-related careers of half of the potential labor force logically has an impact on the overall numbers of information technology professionals, programmers, computers scientists, systems analysts, network designers, software designers, and engineers. Women's attrition from courses that prepare students for cutting-edge careers is disturbing from a national economic perspective; it is also disturbing in terms of what it might portend for women's economic futures. Computer-related careers typically pay well and could substantially boost women's economic status; women's relative disinterest in them threatens to magnify and exacerbate pay gaps. (See "Earned Degrees in Computer Science, Technology, and Engineering Fields, by Sex" on page 58.)[59]

In thinking about women in the work force, the commission underscores that computer science skills will become increasingly integral to many occupations in which they are perhaps being introduced right now. The range of occupations and skills that will be involved in the new computer culture will not be limited to programming and coding. As girls and women think about technological careers, the choice will not be between being a coder or programmer—however important these competencies are—or being out of the game. (See "Distribution of Jobs in Computer and Engineering Fields, by Sex, and Projections of Job Growth in Technology-Related Fields" on page 60.)

Girls Confront the New Economy: Another Case of "We Can, But I Don't Want To"?

The girls in the Foundation's focus groups acknowledge that computers will be central to the 21st-century economy, but approach this fact with resignation rather than enthusiasm. "Basically, your whole future is probably going to be in computers," comments a middle school student from Washington, DC. "It's going to change most of the world," remarks a high school student from Fairfax.

> *In the future, that's all [we're] going to have, so we might as well get used to it now.*
>
> —*Fairfax, Virginia, middle school student*

In addition to a vague conviction that "everything" is going to be computers, girls recognize that computers will be integral to a variety of jobs and occupations. When asked if there would be any job that would not require computer expertise, a student from Washington, DC, says, "Garbage man, and McDonald's."

Girls' ideas about careers mirror their attitudes toward computer science, games, and other dimensions of the computer culture: They assert that they are not

Women in Information Technology Careers

A 1999 survey by computerjobs.com, an online journal for computer professionals, assesses salaries in the field. In doing so, it reflects gender gaps in the profession.

The vast majority (80 percent) of the 32,000 information technology (IT) professionals responding to the survey were men. While respondents were not a statistically representative sample, data reviewed from individual states suggest a similar 4:1 male to female ratio in the IT profession.

The survey found that average earnings by women in the IT field are 85 percent that of men. The report finds it "staggering" that a "historically biased pay scale is still used in the country's most advanced field. … The field, unlike other professions, has no historical salary model to point to as a reason for salary differences, which leaves the salary inequity explanation open for debate." Some female respondents speculated that women may be "afraid to ask for what they are worth" in a field that rewards initiative and often requires negotiation for contract work. In the survey, the salary gap between men and women was unrelated to job experience.

Survey Respondents, by Sex

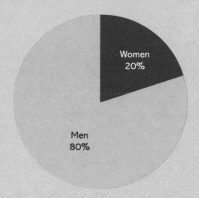

Source: computerjobs.com, 1999

Comparison of IT Salaries, by Sex

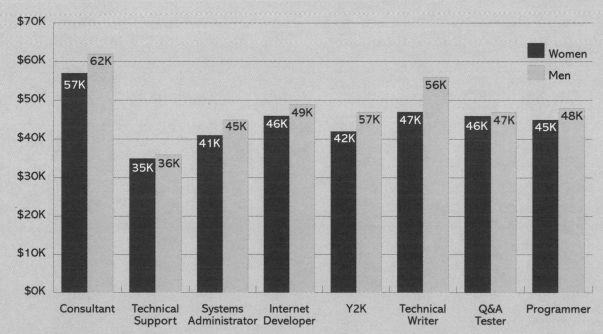

Source: computerjobs.com, 1999

Earned Degrees in Computer Science, Technology, and Engineering Fields, by Sex

According to the U.S. Department of Education, in 1995 women comprised 9 percent of earned bachelor's degrees in engineering-related technologies, 28 percent of earned bachelor's degrees in computer and information sciences, and 17 percent of earned bachelor's degrees in engineering. At the doctoral level, women earned 18 percent of computer and information sciences degrees, 12 percent of engineering degrees, and 11 percent of engineering-related technologies degrees.

In 1993, according to the National Science Foundation (*Women, Minorities, and Persons with Disabilities in Science and Engineering: 1996*), women made up 22 percent of the overall population of computer sciences graduate students.

Earned Degrees in Computer Science, Technology, and Engineering Fields, by Sex, 1995

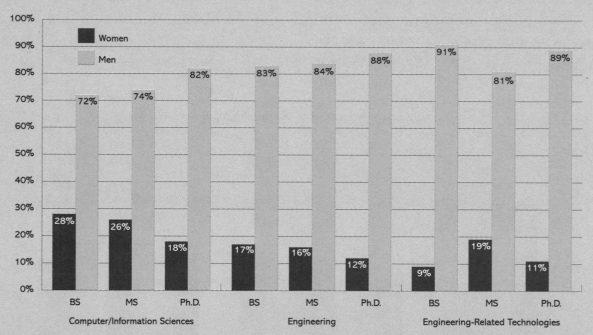

Source: U.S. Department of Education, 1995

anxious about their abilities, but simply lack interest in further study of technology or related careers. Girls do not describe careers in computing as too challenging, mathematically oriented, or demanding. Rather, girls repeatedly say they shun them as unambitious, unchallenging, antisocial, and tedious. Girls can do it, they assert. But I don't want to.[60] A Fairfax, Virginia, middle school girl says, "I think it's kind of a waste of intelligence." A high school girl in Baltimore says she thinks girls choose not to go into technology because "girls like the analytical side, more than just the basic electrical thing."

I don't want to take computer science. It's not so much that I don't like computers, but the program, I guess the language. Just looking at it, all the programming and these funny-looking things on the paper. It [takes] so much stuff to do one thing on the computer.

—Richmond high school student

Commissioner Cornelia Brunner has found that when it comes to careers in high-tech fields, men and women tell the story about their career paths quite differently. Successful men often sound as if they "made up their minds shortly after birth about what they wanted to be and then set about systematically pursuing their career goals by taking all the right courses and landing all the right jobs." Successful women in the same high-tech professions, even those with analogous career paths, typically tell a tale of serendipity, in which they describe having no clear goal and admit to making decisions about courses and jobs based on friendships and the desire to help other people out. They describe themselves as grateful for being given job opportunities even when they doubted their ability to do the work. These differences in career narrative are important because if women only hear male narratives, they can get the impression that in order to be successful in a technical profession, you have to have been "born" to it. Other research suggests that girls have little knowledge of the range of computing career options available, and apparently dichotomize the field into jobs requiring "near-genius" ability or jobs consisting of menial data and word processing.[61]

We have already seen that girls object to computer courses and pursuits because they see them as encouraging a solitary and passive life. They see computer careers in the same way. "I'd rather do something like interacting with people," says one middle school student from Fairfax. "I don't want to sit at a desk all day and use a computer." Says another student, "I'd like a job with people."

Research on girls' perceptions of computer careers is deeply troubling. It demonstrates wide discrepancies in the characteristics women give to their own ideal careers and the characteristics of careers in computing. In recent research, for example, women ranked "making full use of my abilities" as the most important characteristic of their own future career, but ranked it thirteenth on the characteristics of computer fields. In contrast—and in keeping with the "tool/toy" distinction described earlier—women deemed "involvement with new technologies" as the first characteristic of computer careers, yet a distant twelfth on their list of important career characteristics.[62]

Girls level another criticism at computer jobs—that they foster materialism. Girls describe them as doing little for the social good, but simply providing a way to make "big money" fast. Girls also draw a gender distinction here, suggesting that boys are less ambitious and more driven by immediate financial rewards than girls. "Guys are more into it because right now, it's the fastest and easiest way to make money," a Fairfax high school student explains. "It doesn't take a lot. You don't have to have a college degree to do it. All you have to do is take six months of computer

Distribution of Jobs in Computer and Engineering Fields, by Sex, and Projections of Job Growth in Technology-Related Fields

According to a 1996 National Science Foundation study (*Women, Minorities, and Persons with Disabilities in Science and Engineering: 1996*), women constituted 30 percent of the labor force in computer and mathematical sciences occupations in 1993. Of the 720,000 women in these fields, 81 percent were white, 10 percent Asian American, 6 percent African American, and 3 percent Hispanic. Fewer than 1 percent (500) were Native American.

According to U.S. Department of Labor assessments, "information technology jobs are projected to be among the fastest-growing occupations between 1996 and 2006" (U.S. Department of Labor, Bureau of Labor Statistics, *MLR: The Editor's Desk,* October 28, 1998, stats.bls.gov/opub/ted/1998/oct/wk4/art03.htm). The fields most likely to experience a "much faster [than average] rate of growth"—defined as an increase in employment of 36 percent or more— in the next 10 years are the fields in which women are profoundly underrepresented and underenrolled.

The Department of Labor's Occupational Handbook identifies computer scientists, computer engineers, and systems analysts as the top three fastest-growing occupations, and among the top 20 in the number of new jobs created. Computer systems managers, who direct and plan programming, computer operations, and data processing, are expected to be in high demand, along with managers in science and engineering, especially in fields heavily dependent on computer technology. Biotechnology and gene-based sciences, for example, both rely centrally on the innovative use of computer technology.

Computer programming is expected to see a "faster" than average rate of growth (21 percent to 35 percent) over the next 10 years. Finally, the prospects for information technology personnel remain strong, according to the U.S. Department of Labor.

All of these fields are likely to require greater levels of initial and ongoing education. The Department of Labor reports that a bachelor's degree is "virtually a prerequisite" for computer scientists, engineers, and systems analysts. Additionally, professionals in all these fields will need to be highly computer fluent— lifelong learners of rapidly changing technologies.

courses, and I know a lot of guys who have done that. … I think girls want more of a challenge. We've developed a sense that we want to go out there and do something and make a difference, and guys just want to make money."

The reason why you see more men doing computer stuff is that girls are more ambitious than that. My parents always say, "Do something with computers," because it is stable and stuff, but a lot [of people] don't want to be at a desk from 9 to 5. They want to do something more ambitious than that.

—Baltimore middle school student

While acknowledging that "money" was one of the best reasons to pursue computer science careers, girls in another study personally reported having little interest in the field because it did not capture the diversity of their interests and values.[63]

Although girls readily concede that "all jobs" will require computers, they admit that they are unclear about what this means. All of the participants in an African American group in Baltimore feel that they don't really know their career options relative to technology; other groups concede that they are only vaguely aware of the social, interactive, and creative applications of computers. "I think there are jobs where you can work with people in the computer field," argues a Fairfax girl. "We just don't know what they are. We hear about computer programmers and people who sit behind a computer all day, but there are people who go out there, and maybe sell the product, or travel, going to different companies and showing them how to use the programs." This lack of knowledge underscores the positive potential of school counselors. In focus groups, girls say that teachers and counselors give them very little information about these career and course options. This is particularly true for African American and Hispanic women: "I [need] education about careers in computers. If I felt I knew [about] it, I'd do it," comments a high school student in Washington, DC. Counselors and teachers clearly need to be educated about careers that depend on computer fluency, and they need to inform young women who are not college-bound about certification opportunities and vocational programs in information technology.[64]

RECOMMENDATIONS

Develop a better marketing campaign. Girls have a firm notion of what "computer careers" look like, and the picture is distasteful and masculine. They need to know more about the range of career options. The reality is far more complex and diverse than the stereotype.

Impart a more complex, realistic view of jobs. Educators, parents, employers, and guidance counselors need to impart a more complex, realistic view of jobs that rely heavily or centrally on computer technology. Many of these jobs emphasize communication, collaboration, and creativity. Additionally, all students need to learn more about how computer technology is going to transform nontechnical occupations.

Economic incentives are not enough. Girls are getting the message loudly that without training in technology they risk falling behind economically. But this message may not appeal to girls individually, some of whom criticize their peers who are studying information technology as too "materialistic."

Focus on non-college-bound women. Guidance counselors, especially, should focus on presenting information technology career options to young women who may not be college-bound immediately after high school. Some of the better-paying career options in information technology may not require a bachelor's degree but, rather, certification or training experiences during or after high school.

APPENDIX

**Biographies of Commissioners,
Researchers, and Staff**

BIOGRAPHIES OF COMMISSIONERS, RESEARCHERS, AND STAFF

Commissioners

Kathleen Bennett is the founder of the Girls' Middle School in Mountain View, California. The school's innovative educational environment focusing on math, science, engineering, and technology, social and emotional learning, and diversity has been recognized in the *New York Times, Newsweek* and *CBS Sunday Morning News.* Bennett brings more than 30 years of educational and business experience to her role as head of the school. A former middle school teacher, she holds California State teaching credentials in both elementary and secondary education. Her high-tech career as a technical writer, trainer, and HyperCard consultant included work with Apple, GriD, Claris, and Oracle.

Cornelia Brunner is associate director and media designer at the Center for Children and Technology/ Education Development Center in New York City. Brunner, who received her doctorate at Columbia University in 1975, has been involved in the research, production, and teaching of educational technology for 30 years. She has designed educational materials incorporating technologies to support teaching in science, social studies, media literacy, and the arts. Brunner has taught experimental courses at Bank Street College and the Media Workshop in New York, helping teachers learn to integrate technology into their curriculum and use multimedia authoring tools to design their own educational programs. She has written articles including "Gender and Technology" in *Math and Science for Girls: The Complete Proceedings* (1992), and "Gender and Distance Learning" in the *Annals of the American Academy of Political and Social Science* (1991). For the National Science Foundation, she created *Inquire: Software Tools for Science Education* (1988).

Tarah Cherry is an elementary school science teacher at the East Rock Global Magnet School in New Haven, Connecticut. She was a 1994 AAUW Educational Foundation Eleanor Roosevelt Teacher Fellow and a Yale New Haven Teachers' Institute Fellow from 1989 through 1991, in 1993, and in 1997. She received her master's degree in early childhood education from Southern Connecticut State University in 1996 and her bachelor's degree in the same major from Salem State University. Her articles for the Yale University Press include "Afro American Auto-Biography" and "What Makes Airplanes Fly." Her article "The Difficulties in Computer Operations in Large School Districts" was published in *New Moon* magazine for girls (May/June 1998).

James Cooper is the Commonwealth Professor of Education in the Curry School of Education at the University of Virginia, where he served as dean from 1984 to 1994. As dean, he created an innovative five-year program that culminates in the simultaneous awarding of both a bachelor's degree in an academic major and a master of teaching degree. The five-year program has received a $1 million equipment grant from IBM Corporation. Cooper received four degrees from Stanford University—two in history and two in education—including his doctorate in 1967. His numerous books, chapters, journal articles, and monographs address the areas of technology in teacher education, supervision of teachers, and teacher education program evaluation.

Patricia Diaz Dennis is senior vice president and assistant general counsel, regulation and law, for SBC Communications, Inc., the parent company for Southwestern Bell and other subsidiaries, in San Antonio, Texas. She received her law degree from Loyola Marymount University in Los Angeles. Before becoming counsel for SBC, she served as a Reagan appointee on the Federal Communications Commission and the National Labor Relations Board and as a Bush appointee as assistant secretary of state for human rights and humanitarian affairs. Dennis, who received the 1992 Houston YWCA Hispanic Woman of the Year Award, is a trustee for the Radio and Television News Directors Foundation and the Tomás Rivera Policy Institute.

Mae Jemison is founder of the Jemison Institute at Dartmouth College, where she is professor of environmental studies. She received a medical degree from Cornell University, a bachelor of science in chemical engineering, and a bachelor of arts in African and Afro-American Studies from Stanford University. Jemison practiced medicine in a Cambodian refugee camp and in West Africa as a medical officer with the Peace Corps. She was working as a general practitioner in Los Angeles when NASA selected her and 14 others for astronaut training. In 1992 she became the first woman of color to enter space as a mission specialist aboard the shuttle *Endeavor.*

Yasmin Kafai is on the faculty at the UCLA Graduate School of Education & Information Studies where she also heads KIDS (Kids Interactive Design Studios), a research group dedicated to exploring interactive multimedia design environments for young children. She holds a master's and doctorate in education from Harvard University as well as a degree from the Technical University in Berlin, Germany. Her current research focuses on video games as learning environments in children's homes and schools. In the context of home and school, she also studies issues of gender preferences and the design of gender-equitable learning environments. Kafai authored *Minds in Play: Computer Game Design as a Context for Children's Learning* (Lawrence Erlbaum Associates, 1995) and edited *Constructionism in Practice: Designing, Thinking and Learning in a Digital World* (Lawrence Erlbaum Associates, 1996). She has also written articles on computer and information science. She was a postdoctoral fellow and research assistant at the MIT Media Laboratory for five years.

Marcia C. Linn is professor of development and cognition in the Graduate School of Education at the University of California, Berkeley. A fellow of the American Association for the Advancement of Science, she researches science learning, gender equity, and the design of technological learning environments. Her publications include *Computers, Teachers, Peers: Science Learning Partners,* with Sherry Hsi (Lawrence Erlbaum Associates, 2000); *Toward a Psychology of Gender,* with Janet Hyde (Hopkins, 1986); and *Designing Pascal Solutions,* with M. C. Clancy (W.H. Freeman, 1992). For her work in gender equity she received the American Educational Research Association's Willystine Goodsell Award in

1991. Linn earned her bachelor of arts in psychology and statistics and her doctorate in educational psychology from Stanford University.

Jane Metcalfe is president and co-founder of *Wired* magazine and its new "cyberstation" HotWired, based in San Francisco. She received her bachelor's degree, with honors, in international affairs from the University of Colorado. Prior to forming *Wired*, she worked at *Electric Word* magazine, an Amsterdam-based magazine covering such leading-edge technologies as machine translation, optical character recognition, and speech recognition. In 1994 Metcalfe was named Co-Journalist of the Year (along with *Wired* co-founder Louis Rossetto) by the Northern California Chapter of the Society of Professional Journalists. In 1994 she was elected to the board of the Electronic Frontier Foundation.

Eli Noam is a professor of finance and economics at Columbia University and the director of the Columbia Institute for Tele-Information (CITI). He received his bachelor's, doctorate, and law degree from Harvard University and has focused his research on the economics and management of media, information, and communications. He has served as New York State public service commissioner, regulating the telecommunications and energy industries. His numerous books and articles include a series on global telecommunications and on the cybermedia of the future. Recent books include *Telecommunications in Africa* (Oxford University Press, 1999) and *Interconnecting the Network of Networks*. Noam was a member of the advisory boards for the federal government's FTS-2000 telecommunications network, the IRS's computer system reorganization, and the National Computer Systems Laboratory. He is currently developing web-based courses for distance education.

Cynthia Samuels is the senior national editor at National Public Radio. Previously, she was president and chief executive officer of Cobblestone Productions Online and On Television, in Malibu, California. Samuels, who received her bachelor's from Smith College, began her career as an assistant in the Washington bureau of *CBS News*. She worked as a documentary researcher for KQED's pioneering series *News Room* and as assistant foreign editor and deputy New York bureau manager for CBS. She became the political and planning producer for NBC's *Today* show, where she spent nine years covering politics, family issues, and rock 'n roll. Samuels has been a producer for the Third Annual Children's Interactive Media Festival and a consultant for EXCITE! search engine, CYBERLIFE, Discovery Channel, and McGraw Hill Home Interactive.

Aliza Sherman is president of Cybergrrl, Inc., a media and entertainment company creating popular online content, virtual communities, and resources for women, and founder of Webgrrls, a networking group for women interested in the Internet. Webgrrls has more than 100 chapters worldwide. She is also a freelance writer whose work has appeared in *USA Today, Ms., Self,* and *Executive Female.* Sherman is the author of *Cybergrrl: A Woman's Guide to the World Wide Web* (Ballantine Books, 1998). In 1997 she was named one of "The Most Powerful People in Their 20's" by *Swing* magazine and listed as one of the "Top 50 People Who Matter Most on the Internet" by *Newsweek.*

Sherry Turkle is a professor of sociology at the Massachusetts Institute of Technology. She received her doctorate from Harvard University and has written numerous articles on psychoanalysis and culture as well as the "subjective side" of people's relationships with technology, especially computers. She is the author of *The Second Self: Computers and the Human Spirit* (Simon and Schuster, 1984) and more recently *Life on the Screen: Identity in the Age of the Internet* (Touchstone Books, 1997). Turkle has pursued her work on the computer culture with support from the National Science Foundation and the MacArthur Foundation. Her work on computers and people has been reported in *Time, Newsweek, U.S. News & World Report, People,* and *USA Today,* and she has been a guest on numerous radio and television shows, including *Nightline,* NBC's *Today* show, *20/20, CBS Morning/Evening News, Dateline,* and *The Jane Pauley Show.*

Jane Walters is executive director of Partners in Public Education. She received her doctorate in school administration from Duke University, her master's in counseling from the University of Memphis, and her bachelor's degree from the School of Music and Music History at Rhodes College. She holds a professional teaching certificate in guidance, mathematics, music, and school administration.

Researchers

Dorothy Bennett is senior project manager at the Center for Children and Technology of the Education Development Center. She has 12 years' experience in the research and development of educational media, curricula, and teacher enhancement programs. Projects she has helped develop include the Telementoring project (an Internet-based mentoring project for high school girls) and the Imagination Place Project, an online design space for middle schoolers. Formerly, she was a researcher at the Children's Television Workshop's mathematics series, *SQUARE ONE TV.* She received her master's in education from Bank Street College of Education, with a focus on adolescent development.

Sherry Hsi is a postdoctoral scholar at the Center for Innovative Learning Technologies at the University of California, Berkeley, synthesizing and advancing research on low-cost computing and computer-mediated learning. She is also a member of the faculty for the Virtual High School Cooperative at the Concord Consortium in Concord, Massachusetts. Hsi received her bachelor's, master's, and doctorate in science and mathematics education from the University of California, Berkeley. She sits on the editorial board for the *Journal of the Learning Sciences* and reviews articles for the *Journal of Women and Minorities in Science and in Engineering.* She has conducted gender studies in engineering education, spatial reasoning instruction, and middle school science. She is the co-author of *Computers, Teachers, Peers: Science Learning Partners* (Lawrence Erlbaum Associates, 2000); "Productive Discussion in Science: Gender Equity Through Electronic Discourse" in the *Journal of Science Education and Technology* (1997); and "Lifelong Science Learning on the Internet: Knowledge Integration Environment" with M.C. Linn and P. Bell (forthcoming).

Celinda Lake is president of Lake Snell Perry and Associates, a national opinion research firm located in Washington, DC. Lake earned her master's degree in political science and survey research from the University of Michigan at Ann Arbor and a certificate in political science from the University of Geneva. She received her undergraduate degree from Smith College. A nationally recognized expert on the women's vote and women's candidacies, she is one of the leading strategists for the Democratic Party and democratic parties in Eastern Europe and South Africa. Prior to forming LSPA, she was a partner in Mellman-Lazarus-Lake and Greenberg-Lake, political director of the Women's Campaign Fund, and research director for the Institute for Social Research in Ann Arbor. She wrote *Public Opinion Polling: A Manual for Special Interest Groups* (Island Press, 1987).

Kathleen Moore is project manager for the Educational Research Division of Gordon S. Black Corporation. She received her master's degree and doctorate in psychology from the University of Missouri–Columbia and earned her bachelor's in psychology cum laude from the University of Rochester. She has 15 years of experience in higher education, including work as an adjunct professor at several colleges and as a researcher and administrator in counseling and testing at a large community college.

Staff

Anthony Capitos served as librarian and archivist for the AAUW Educational Foundation from 1997 to fall 1999, when he became a librarian for the U.S. Defense Mapping Agency.

Pamela Haag is director of research for the AAUW Educational Foundation.

Karen Sloan Lebovich is director of the AAUW Educational Foundation She directs its fellowship, grant, and research programs; oversees its development and fundraising programs; and manages the Foundation's $120 million in assets.

Priscilla Little is the former director of research at the AAUW Educational Foundation.

ENDNOTES

ENDNOTES

[1] See AAUW Educational Foundation, *Gender Gaps: Where Schools Still Fail Our Children* (Washington, DC: AAUW Educational Foundation, 1998). Please see sidebars throughout this report for additional statistics on girls and women in computer courses, majors, and careers.

[2] The AAUW Educational Foundation commissioned Lake Snell Perry and Associates to conduct seven focus groups with 70 middle and high school girls to discuss their views on computer technology in the home, school, and workplace. These groups, held with girls from urban and suburban communities in Baltimore, Maryland; Richmond, Virginia; Washington, DC; and Fairfax County, Virginia, probed girls' ideas about software design, their views of gender differences in computer use, and, among other things, their opinions about the status of computer technology in the next century. To further ensure a diverse perspective, groups were conducted with white, African American, Asian American, and Hispanic girls.

Harris Interactive, a survey research firm, was commissioned to conduct an online survey of 892 teachers concerning their current and projected use of computer technology in the classroom, their experiences with computer technology in teacher education, their best and worst moments with computer technology, their ideas about the future classroom, and their perspectives on learning dynamics in the tech-rich classroom. Because teachers polled were at least "tech-savvy" enough to access and complete an online survey, they represent "high end" users among K-12 educators.

The AAUW Educational Foundation commissioned three original review essays to support the commission's deliberations. Researcher Cornelia Brunner of the Education Development Center wrote an overview essay on the computer culture, Sherry Hsi reviewed gender and software, and researcher Dorothy Bennett, also of the Education Development Center, reviewed insights for teachers from cutting-edge research on gender and computer technology.

Finally, this report synthesizes and reviews much of the existing research on technology, gender, and education. It draws especially on national studies, but reviews smaller qualitative studies and data as well.

[3] The commission's efforts to facilitate girls' entry into computing careers follow the lead of a group of women who have been working for many years on this issue. They include, among many others, Anita Borg (IWT), Barbara Simons (ACM), Carol Muller (MentorNet), Maria Klawe (UBC), and Suzanne Brainard (UW WISE). Commissioner Kathleen Bennett brought their activities and achievements to the fore in the commission's discussions.

[4] For the distinction between the instrumental computer—the computer that does things for us—and the subjective computer that does things to us as people, see Sherry Turkle, *The Second Self: Computers and the Human Spirit* (New York: Simon and Schuster, 1984) and Turkle, *Life on the Screen: Identity in the Age of the Internet* (New York: Touchstone, 1997).

[5] See Sherry Turkle, "Computational Reticence: Why Women Fear the Intimate Machine," in Cheris Kramarae, ed., *Technology and Women's Voices* (New York: Routledge, 1988). The literature on gender and the computer culture is extensive. For example, see Cornelia Brunner, "Technology and Gender: Differences in Masculine and Feminine Views," *NASSP Bulletin* 81 (November 1997); Brunner, "Technology Perceptions by Gender," *Education Digest* 63 (February 1998); Sara Kiesler, "Pool Halls, Chips, and War Games: Women in the Culture of Computing," *Psychology of Women Quarterly* 9 (December 1985); Sherry Turkle and Seymour Papert, "Epistemological Pluralism: Styles and Voices within the Computer Culture," *Signs* 16, no. 1 (1990); Ellen Tarlin, "Computers in the Classrooms: Where Are All the Girls?" *Harvard Educational Review, Focus Series,* no. 3 (1997); Margaret Honey, "The Maternal Voice in the Technological Universe," in Donna Bassin, Margaret Honey, and Meryle Mahrer Kaplan, eds., *Representations of Motherhood* (New Haven: Yale University Press, 1994), pp. 220-39; Sherry Turkle,

The Second Self; Zoe Sofia, "The Mythic Machine: Gendered Irrationalities and Computer Culture," in Hank Bromley and Michael Apple, eds., *Education/Technology/Power: Educational Computing as Social Practice* (Albany: SUNY Press, 1998); Nancy Knupfer, "Gender Divisions across Technology Advertisements and the WWW," *Theory into Practice* 37, no. 1 (1998); Matthew Weinstein, "Computer Advertising and the Construction of Gender," in Bromley and Apple, eds., *Education/Technology/Power.*

[6] Additionally, although 70 percent of school computers are capable of running Windows or Mac OS, more than half of them cannot efficiently run multimedia applications. And although 48 percent of computers are now found in classrooms rather than computer labs, only 18 percent of instructional rooms have Internet access. See Ronald Anderson and Amy Ronnkvist, "The Presence of Computers in American Schools," in *Teaching, Learning, and Computing: 1998 National Survey,* Center for Research on Information Technology and Organizations (1999) [www.crito.uci.edu/TLC/findings/].

[7] Anderson and Ronnkvist, "The Presence of Computers in American Schools"; Pamela Mendels, "Crumbling Schools Have Trouble Getting Online," *New York Times,* February 24, 2000. Some studies suggest that disadvantages within schools and classes according to student poverty or low community income may not have as much to do with the infusion of technology itself but, rather, with how the technology is used, and the sorts of learning it supports. An Educational Testing Service (ETS) study using national data concludes that on indicators that appear to be unrelated or only weakly related to higher mathematics achievement—i.e., student "frequency of use"—social inequalities by class have been remedied or diminished. However, where computers do appear related to achievement outcomes—for example, in their use for "higher order" learning and the availability of intensive teacher education for computer technology—poor and minority students are indeed at a material disadvantage. Another study from the Teaching, Learning, Computing project finds that within demographically heterogeneous schools, Internet use favors high-ability classes. Educational Testing Service, *Does It Compute?: The Relationship between Educational Technology and Student Achievement in Mathematics* (Princeton, NJ: ETS, 1998); Henry Becker et. al., "The Equity Threat of

Promising Innovations: Pioneering Internet-Connected Schools," *Journal of Educational Computing Research* 19, no. 1 (1998); R. Kozma and R. Croninger, "Technology and the Fate of At-Risk Students," *Education and Urban Society* 24, no. 4 (1992).

[8] *Education Week* in collaboration with the Milken Exchange on Education Technology, *Technology Counts '99: Building the Digital Curriculum* (Washington, DC: Editorial Projects in Education, 1999).

[9] The projection of teacher hiring and needs is from Richard Riley, U.S. Secretary of Education, cited in Rebecca Jones, "The Kids are Coming: Schools Nationwide Brace for the Biggest Enrollment Boom Ever," *American School Board Journal,* April 1997, pp. 21-24.

[10] Cornelia Brunner, "Technology, Gender, and Education: Defining the Problem," prepared for the AAUW Educational Foundation's Commission on Technology, Gender, and Teacher Education, 1998. On the teacher's influence over students' perceptions and use of information technology, see Larry Cuban, "High-Tech Schools and Low-Tech Teaching: A Commentary," *Journal of Computing in Teacher Education* 14, no. 2 (1998); Cuban, *Teachers and Machines: The Classroom Use of Technology Since 1920* (New York: Teachers College Press, 1986); Barry Fishman, "Student Traits and the Use of Computer-Mediated Communication Tools: What Matters and Why," paper delivered at the American Educational Research Association annual meeting, San Diego, 1998; Fishman, "Characteristics of Students Related to Computer-Mediated Communications Activity," *Journal of Research on Computing in Education* 32, no. 1 (1999).

[11] A 1998 survey found that almost all reported using word processing, but generally "never" or "seldom" used spreadsheets or databases. CD-ROM and Internet use fell in a middle range. Caryl Sheffield, "An Examination of Self-Reported Computer Literacy Skills of Preservice Teachers," *Action in Teacher Education* 17, no. 4 (1996); Elizabeth Kirby, "Developing Instructional Technology Curricula for Preservice Teachers: A Longitudinal Assessment of Entry Skills," paper presented at the American Educational Research Association annual meeting, San Diego, 1998.

[12] On teacher attitudes and practices with information technology, see Stephen Kerr, "Lever and Fulcrum: Educational Technology in Teachers' Thoughts and Practices," *Teachers College Record* 93, no. 1 (1991); Cuban, "High-Tech Schools and Low-Tech Teaching"; Sara Dexter and Ronald Anderson, "Teachers' Views of Computers as Catalysts for Change in Their Teaching Practice," *Journal of Research on Computing in Education* 31, no. 3 (1999); David Pugalee and Rich Robinson, "A Study of the Impact of Teacher Training in Using Internet Resources for Mathematics and Science Instruction," *Journal of Research on Computing in Education* 31, no. 1 (1998); Karen Ferneding-Lenert, "The 'Inevitable' Diffusion of Technology: Reclaiming Teachers' Voices," paper presented at the American Educational Research Association annual meeting, San Diego, 1998.

[13] *Technology Counts '99;* See Linda Darling-Hammond, "What Matters Most: A Competent Teacher for Every Child," *Phi Delta Kappan* 78, no. 3 (1996); Darling-Hammond, "The Quiet Revolution: Rethinking Teacher Development," *Educational Leadership* 53, no. 6 (1996).

[14] According to a recent report by the National Council for Accreditation of Teacher Education (NCATE), "having a written and funded technology plan, while rare, has only a low correlation" with greater use of technology by student teachers, as does formal IT coursework. An "integrated model," in contrast, would appear to make a substantial change in pedagogy and course structure. Educational Testing Service, *Does It Compute?;* NCATE, *Technology and the New Professional Teacher* (Washington, DC: NCATE, 1997); International Society for Technology in Education, *Will New Teachers Be Prepared to Teach in the Digital Age? National Survey on Information Technology in Teacher Education* (Santa Monica, CA: Milken Exchange on Education Technology, 1999); David Pepi, "The Emperor's New Computer: A Critical Look at our Appetite for Computer Technology," *Journal of Teacher Education* 47, no. 3 (1996).

[15] Sherry Hsi, "Supporting Gender Equity through Design: Research Review and Synthesis for AAUW Educational Foundation," prepared for the AAUW Educational Foundation's Commission on Technology, Gender, and Teacher Education, 1998.

[16] Marcia Linn and Sherry Hsi, *Computers, Teachers, Peers: Science Learning Partners* (New Jersey: Lawrence Erlbaum Associates, 2000).

[17] The majority of the 417 respondents surveyed for this report who described their "best experience using computer technology" in response to an open-ended question point to a lesson that utilized computer technology successfully to support students' writing, research, or publishing efforts. Several recall instances when they used PowerPoint to make a presentation or had their students create colorful presentations of lessons and material for the curriculum.

[18] Jupiter Communications, "Digital Kids Online," *Edutainment Monthly* 25 (March 1997). See Brunner, "Technology, Gender, and Education."

[19] Another image of the classroom of tomorrow emphasizes an increased use of virtual classrooms. One teacher, who predicts that "classrooms and school buildings as we know them will be a distant memory," elaborates that "students will have personalized, individually designed curriculum ... and the learning site will be the home." Because computer technology makes possible "portable" learning, this teacher further believes that "service learning and more actual on-the-job training will become the norm, as in former eras when apprenticeships were honored ways to pass on knowledge and experience."

[20] Commissioner Brunner writes that the emphasis on communication and collaboration "is not only important to the education reform agenda, but will also ensure that learning contexts are responsive to the needs of all learners, not just those who resonate with prevailing notions of technology as an information storehouse." See Brunner, "Technology, Gender, and Education." An emphasis on the development of critical thinking skills, problem-solving abilities, and the application of the curriculum to meaningful, real-life problems are some of the characteristics of a "constructivist" approach to learning. On teacher attitudes about pedagogy and constructivist learning styles as influenced by computer technology, see findings and snapshots from the National Science Foundation-funded *Teaching, Learning, and Computing,* especially Henry Jay Becker, "Internet Use by Teachers: Conditions of Professional Use and Teacher-Directed Student Use, Report no. 1"

[www.crito.uci.edu/TLC/findings/Internet-Use/startpage.htm].

21 National Research Council, Computer Science and Telecommunications Board, *Being Fluent with Information Technology* (Washington, DC: National Academy Press, 1999). On information technology in the science curriculum, see Marcia Linn et. al., "Using the Internet to Enhance Student Understanding of Science: The Knowledge Integration Environment," in *Interactive Learning Environments* (in press).

22 On the significance of these factors to outcomes, see among others, David Dwyer, "Apple Classrooms of Tomorrow: What We've Learned," *Educational Leadership* 51, no. 7 (1996); Richard Coley et. al., Educational Testing Service, *Computers and Classrooms: The Status of Technology in U.S. Schools* (Princeton, NJ: Educational Testing Service, 1996); Barbara Means, ed., *Technology and Education Reform: The Reality Behind the Promise* (San Francisco: Jossey-Bass Publishers, 1994); American Institutes of Research, for the U.S. Department of Education, "Toward Assessing the Effectiveness of Using Technology in K-12 Education" (Washington, DC: American Institutes of Research, 1997); The Benton Foundation, "The Learning Connection: Will the Information Highway Transform Schools and Prepare Students for the 21st Century?" (Washington, DC: Benton Foundation, 1996) [www.benton.org/library]; Jan Hawkins, "Technology in Education: Transitions," Education Development Center, Center for Children and Technology (1997); Erik Strommen and Bruce Lincoln, "Constructivism, Technology, and the Future of Classroom Learning," *Education and Urban Society* 24, no. 4 (1992).

23 Julie Nicholson, et al., "Influences of Gender and Open-Ended Software on First Graders' Collaborative Composing Activities on Computers," *Journal of Computing in Childhood Education* 9, no. 1 (1998); Gail Crombie and Patrick Armstrong, "Effects of Classroom Gender Composition on Adolescents' Computer-Related Attitudes and Future Intentions," *Journal of Educational Computing Research* 20, no. 4 (1999); Geoffrey Underwood, "Gender Differences and Effects of Co-Operation in a Computer-Based Language Task," *Educational Research* 36, no. 1 (1994); Tor Busch, "Gender, Group Composition, Cooperation, and Self-Efficacy in Computer Studies," *Journal of Educational Computing Research* 14, no. 2

(1997); Janet Schofield, *Computers and Classroom Culture* (New York: Cambridge University Press, 1995); Rod Corson, "Gender and Social Facilitation Effects on Computer Competence and Attitudes toward Computers," *Journal of Educational Computing Research* 14, no. 2 (1996).

24 Brad Huber, "I Like Computers, But Many Girls Don't: Gender and Sociocultural Contexts of Computing," in Bromley and Apple, eds., *Education/Technology/Power;* Caroline Eastman, "Accommodating Diversity in Computer Science Education," in Sue Rosser, ed., *Teaching the Majority: Breaking the Gender Barrier in Science, Math, and Engineering* (New York: Teachers University Press, 1995); Linn and Hsi, *Computers, Teachers, Peers.*

25 Lorraine Culley, "Gender Equity and Computing in Secondary Schools: Issues and Strategies for Teachers," in *Computers into Classrooms: More Questions Than Answers* (London: Falmer Press, 1993).

26 Additional findings include the following: Forty-one percent of male teachers think that male students "use technology more freely and frequently," and 28 percent think that female students do. In contrast, 41 percent of male teachers feel that female students are "more fearful of making mistakes with the computer," while only 9 percent believe males to be more so.

27 Huber, "I Like Computers, But Many Girls Don't"; Schofield, *Computers and Classroom Culture;* John Beynon, "Computer Dominant Boys and Invisible Girls," in *Computers into Classrooms: More Questions than Answers;* Elizabeth Arch, "Structured and Unstructured Exposure to Computers: Sex Differences in Attitudes Among College Students," *Sex Roles* 20, no. 5/6 (1989).

28 School spending on software continues to increase, from $670 million in 1996 to $822 million in 1998. Software publishers, according to one report, are breaking up programs into "modules so that they can more easily be used to supplement than replace curricula." According to the most recent national survey of teachers, 53 percent use computer software. Charlene Blohm, *Software Publishers Association Education Market Report* (Washington, DC: Software Publishers Association, 1997); *Technology Counts '99.* On the interrelationship between educational software and games, see Dorothy Bennett, "Inviting Girls

into Technology: Developing Good Educational Practices," prepared for the AAUW Educational Foundation's Commission on Technology, Gender, and Teacher Education, 1999.

[29] Carol Hodes, "Gender Representations in Mathematics Software," *Journal of Educational Technology Systems* 21, no. 1 (1995-96); Barbara Levin, "Children's Views of Technology: The Role of Age, Gender, and School Setting," *Journal of Computing in Childhood Education* 8, no. 4 (1997); Karen Birahimah, "The Non-Neutrality of Educational Computer Software," *Computer Education* 20, no. 4 (1993).

[30] J.C. Herz, "Girls Just Want to Have Fun: When It Comes to Children's Software, Barbie Rules," *New York Times Book Review,* February 14, 1999; see Brunner, "Technology, Gender, and Education.".

[31] Yasmin Kafai, "Video Game Designs by Girls and Boys: Variability and Consistency of Gender Differences," in Justine Cassell and Henry Jenkins, eds., *From Barbie to Mortal Kombat: Gender and Computer Games* (Cambridge, MA: MIT Press, 1998).

[32] For example, teachers note that when software depicts traditional family structures that don't reflect students' life experiences, students regard the software as coming from another world—an issue of social equity in computing that goes beyond the purview of this report.

[33] Hsi, "Supporting Gender Equity through Design"; Software Publishers Association; EvaluTech "Criteria for Evaluation" CD ROMs, www.sret.sreb.org.

[34] Maria Klawe found that boys, in fact, have a range of interests in games, and while violent games are popular, many boys prefer games that challenge them mentally. See Maria Klawe et. al., "Exploring Common Conceptions About Boys and Electronic Games," *The Journal of Computers in Mathematics and Science Teaching* 14, no. 4 (1995). See Kafai, "Video Game Designs by Girls and Boys"; Kafai, *Minds in Play: Computer Game Design as a Context for Children's Learning* (Hillsdale, NJ: Lawrence Erlbaum Associates, 1995); Kafai, "Gender Differences in Children's Constructions of Video Games," in Patricia Greenfield and Rodney Cocking, eds., *Interacting with Video* (Greenwich, CT: Ablex Publishing Corporation, 1995); Kafai and Mitchel

Resnick, eds., *Constructionism in Practice: Designing, Thinking, and Learning in a Digital World* (Mahwah, NJ: Lawrence Erlbaum Associates, 1996); Cornelia Brunner et. al., "Girls' Games and Technological Desire," in *From Barbie to Mortal Kombat*; Andee Rubin et. al., "What Kinds of Educational Computer Games Would Girls Like?" paper presented at the American Educational Research Association annual meeting, Boston, April 1997 [www.terc.edu/mathequity/gw/html/MITpaper.html].

[35] On game characteristics, see Rubin, "What Kind of Educational Computer Games Would Girls Like?"; K.R. Inkpen et. al., "'We Have Never-Forgetful Flowers in Our Garden': Girls' Responses to Electronic Games," *The Journal of Computers in Mathematics and Science Teaching* 13, no. 4 (1994); J. Mokros, Andee Rubin et al., "Where's the Math in Computer Games?" *Hands On!* 21, no. 2 (1998); M.J. Murray and M. Kliman, "Beyond Point and Click," *ENC Focus* (Washington, DC: Eisenhower National Clearinghouse, in press); M.J. Murray, J. Mokros, and Andee Rubin, "Promoting Mathematically Rich, Equitable Game Software," in *Mathematics Teaching in the Middle School* (Washington, DC: National Council of Teachers of Mathematics, in press).

[36] These findings are consistent with other research. While more boys than girls made positive comments about the sound and graphics in games, girls were often particularly invested in a game in which they could "design" some aspect of the characters—for example, their looks or personality. (Boys, in contrast, expressed interest in design primarily when it involved designing inanimate objects such as machines.). Rubin, "What Kind of Educational Computer Games Would Girls Like?" See Bennett, "Inviting Girls into Technology," for a summary of research on girls and games.

[37] Anne L. Davidson and Janet W. Schofield, "Female Voices in Virtual Reality: Drawing Young Girls into an Online World," in K.A. Renninger and W. Shumer, eds., *Building Virtual Communities: Learning and Change in Cyberspace* (New York: Cambridge University Press, in press).

[38] Chris Hancock and Scot Osterweil, "Zoombinis and the Art of Mathematical Play," Technology Education Research Center, 1996 [www.terc.edu/handson/s96/zoom.html]; Rubin,

"What Kind of Educational Computer Games Would Girls Like?" See Hsi, "Supporting Gender Equity through Design" for a review of these programs.

[39] Hsi, "Supporting Gender Equity through Design"; Hsi, "Facilitating Knowledge Integration in Science through Electronic Discussion: The Multimedia Forum Kiosk," Ph.D. diss., University of California, Berkeley (1997).

[40] Janet Schofield, "Teachers, Computer Tutors, and Teaching: The Artificially Intelligent Tutor as an Agent for Classroom Change," *American Educational Research Journal* 31, no. 3 (1994). Among other qualities, the GP Tutor encouraged multiple learning styles and levels of expertise; helped to integrate computer technology into geometry, a subject that is not "about" computer technology, per se; helped to coordinate different mathematics ability levels in the classroom, as it allowed for self-paced learning; and diminished the prohibitive consequences of students confessing to a lack of understanding. Further, the tutor allowed teachers to dispense assistance and help on a more individualized and private basis. These factors made computer technology in this example a valuable partner for better and more equitable learning.

[41] For a brief summary of the ENAIC story, see Kiesler, "Pool Halls, Chips, and War Games"; National Science Foundation, *Women, Minorities, and Persons with Disabilities in Science and Engineering* [NSF 99-338] (Arlington, VA: National Science Foundation, 1999); National Center for Education Statistics, *The 1994 High School Transcript Study Tabulations: Comparative Data on Credits Earned and Demographics for 1994, 1990, 1987, and 1982 High School Graduates* [NCES 97-260] (Washington, DC: Department of Education, 1997); C. Dianne Martin, ed., *In Search of Gender-Free Paradigms for Computer Science* (Washington, DC: International Society for Technology in Education: 1992); Heinrich Stumpf and Julian Stanley, "The Gender Gap in Advanced Placement Computer Science: Participation and Performance, 1984-1996," *The College Board Review*, 1997, p. 181; Rosemary Sutton, "Equity and Computers in Schools: A Decade of Research," *Review of Educational Research* 61, no. 4 (1991); Henry Becker et. al., "Equity in School Computer Use: National Data and Neglected Considerations," *Journal of Educational Computing Research* 3, pp. 289-311; Marcia Linn, "Gender Equity in Computer Learning

Environments," *Computers and the Social Sciences* 1, pp. 19-27; Marlaine Lockheed, *Evaluation of Computer Literacy at the High School Level* (Princeton: Evaluation of Computer Services, 1982).

[42] Garnett Foundation, The Backyard Project, "Encouraging Young Women to Pursue Careers in Computer Science" (California: Global Strategy Group, Inc., 1997); Alan Durndell, "Gender and Computing: A Decade of Change?" *Computers and Education* 28 (January 1997); Jane Margolis, "Geek Mythology: Impact of Computing Culture on the Attraction and Retention of Women Students in Computer Science," working paper of the Carnegie Mellon Project on Gender and Computer Science, in "Women in Computer Sciences" series, 1998; Margolis, "Computing for a Purpose: Gender and Attachment of Computer Science," working paper of the Carnegie Mellon Project on Gender and Computer Science, in "Women in Computer Sciences: Closing the Gender Gap in Higher Education" series. For a brief description of women in computer science, see D.W. Gurer, "Pioneering Women in Computer Science," *Communications of the ACM* 38, no. 1 (1995), pp. 45-54.

[43] On pedagogy and teaching style, see Elliot Soloway and James Spohrer, *Studying the Novice Programmer* (New Jersey: Lawrence Erlbaum Associates, 1989). On learning styles and the computer science curriculum see Dorothy Bennett, *Voices of Women in Engineering* (New York: Education Development Center, Center for Children and Technology, May 1996); Margolis, "Computing for a Purpose"; Turkle and Papert, "Epistemological Pluralism: Styles and Voices within the Computer Culture"; Sue Rosser, *Female Friendly Science: Applying Women's Studies Methods and Theories to Attract Students* (New York: Pergamon Press, 1990); Seymour Papert, "Computer Criticism and Technocratic Thinking," *Educational Researcher* 16, no. 1 (1987); Turkle, "Computational Reticence."

[44] Peggy Newton and Evi Beck, "Computing: An Ideal Occupation for Women?" in *Computers into Classrooms: More Questions Than Answers*; Lola Belle Smith, "The Socialization of Excelling Women with Regard to Technology Careers: Guides and Pathbreakers," Ph.D. diss., University of Georgia (1999); Suzanne Silvermann, *Building Their Future II: High School Girls in Technology Education in Connecticut*

(Hartford, CT: Vocational Equity Research, Training and Evaluation Center, 1998). On classroom examples, see Schofield, *Computers and Classroom Culture.*

45 Susan Chipman and V.G. Thomas, "The Participation of Women and Minorities in Mathematical, Scientific, and Technical Fields," in Ernst Rothkopf, ed., *Review of Research in Education* 14 (Washington, DC: American Educational Research Association, 1987), pp. 387-430; Sue Maple and Frances Stage, "Influences on the Choice of Math/Science Majors by Gender and Ethnicity," *American Educational Research Journal* 28 (Spring 1991), pp. 37-60; Elizabeth Stage, Nancy Kreinberg, et. al., "Increasing the Participation and Achievement of Girls in Math, Science, and Engineering," in Alison Kelly, ed., *Science for Girls* (Philadelphia: Open University Press, 1987), pp. 100-33.

46 Jo Sanders, "Girls and Technology: Villain Wanted," in Rosser, *Teaching the Majority;* James Flowers, *Female Educators and Students Assess Gender Equity in Technology Education: A Survey of Women Involved in Technology Education* (Virginia Vocational Curriculum and Resource Center, 1996), emphasizes the importance of girls who are friends taking computing courses together; Suzanne Silvermann, *Guidance, Gender Equity, and Technology Education* (Hartford, CT: Vocational Equity Research, Training and Evaluation Center, 1998); Silvermann, *Building Their Future II.*

47 Martin, *In Search of Gender-Free Paradigms for Computer Science;* Margolis, "Geek Mythology." The notion of a first-year "filter" class for computer science reprises a pattern in mathematics at the postsecondary level. Marcia Linn and Cathy Kessel interviewed more than 1,500 students interested in mathematics and science, and found that undergraduates complain that courses are designed to "weed out" students rather than "encourage the best to persist." They conclude that the quality of instruction has particular influence over women's decisions to persist, and recommend attention to the development of talent rather than the "filtering out" of students. Similar recommendations may now apply to computer science courses at the secondary and postsecondary level. See Linn and Kessel, "Success in Mathematics: Increasing Talent and Gender Diversity Among College Majors," in J. Kaput, A. Schoenfeld, and E. Dubinsky, eds., *Research in Collegiate Mathematics Education,* vol. 2 (Providence, RI: American Mathematical Society, 1996).

48 Jo Sanders, in "Girls and Technology: Villain Wanted," notes that a critical mass of girlfriends, rather than simply girls, encourages participation in advanced computer classes.

49 See Turkle, "Computational Reticence"; Schofield, *Computers and Classroom Culture.*

50 Brunner, "Technology, Gender, and Education"; Schofield, *Computers and Classroom Culture;* Bennett, *Voices of Women in Engineering.*

51 U.S. Department of Commerce, *Falling through the Net: New Data on the Digital Divide* (Washington, DC: Department of Commerce, 1998); Anderson and Ronnkvist, "The Presence of Computers in American Schools"; Melissa Mangione, "Understanding the Critics of Educational Technology: Gender Inequities and Computers," National Convention of the Association for Educational Communications and Technology Conference, Anaheim, CA (1995); Henry Becker, "Running to Catch a Moving Train: Schools and Information Technologies," *Theory into Practice* 37, no. 1 (1998); Educational Testing Service, *Does It Compute?*

52 Kaiser Family Foundation, *Kids and Media @ the New Millennium: A Comprehensive National Analysis of Children's Media Use* (Menlo Park, CA: Kaiser Family Foundation, 1999).

53 Department of Commerce, *Falling through the Net;* Lily Shashaani, "Socioeconomic Status, Parents' Sex-Role Stereotypes, and the Gender Gap in Computing," *Journal of Research on Computing in Education* 26 (Summer 1994); Dirk Spennemann, "Gender Imbalances in Computer Access among Environmental Science Students," *Journal of Instructional Science and Technology* 1, no. 2 (March 1996).

54 Cassell and Jenkins, eds., *From Barbie to Mortal Kombat;* A. Dorothy Sakamoto, "Video Games Use and the Development of Socio-Cognitive Abilities in Children: Three Surveys of Elementary School Students," *Journal of Applied Social Psychology* 24 (1994), pp. 21-24; Robert Kraut et. al., "HomeNet: A Field Trial of Residential Internet Services," *HomeNet*

1 (1995), pp. 1-8; Janice Woodrow, "The Development of Computer-Related Attitudes of Secondary Students," *Journal of Educational Computing Research* 11, no. 4 (1994), pp. 307-38; Sutton, "Equity and Computers in Schools," pp. 475-503; S.M. Chambers and V.A. Clarke, "Is Inequity Cumulative? The Relationship between Disadvantaged Group Membership and Students' Computing Experience, Knowledge, Attitudes, and Intentions," *Journal of Educational Computing Research* 5, no. 1 (1987), p. 513; Milton Chen, "Gender and Computers: The Beneficial Effects of Experience on Attitudes," *Journal of Educational Computing Research* 2, no. 3 (1986), pp. 265-82; Robert Hess and Irene Miura, "Gender Differences in Enrollment in Computer Camps and Classes," *Sex Roles* 13 (1985), pp. 193-203.

55 Arch, "Structured and Unstructured Exposure to Computers."

56 Schofield, *Computers and Classroom Culture;* Janet Schofield and Anne L. Davidson, "The Internet and Equality of Educational Opportunity," in T. Ottoman and I. Tomek, eds., *Proceedings of ED_MEDIA and ED-TELECOM 98* (Charlottesville, VA: Association for the Advancement of Computing in Education, 1998).

57 Jane Kahle and Judith Meece, "Research on Gender Issues in the Classroom," in D. Gavel, ed., *Handbook of Research on Science Teaching and Learning* (New York: Macmillan, 1994), pp. 542-57; Kafai, "Video Game Designs by Girls and Boys"; Brunner, "Girls' Games and Technological Desire."

58 See McKinsey and Company, *Connecting K-12 Schools to the Information Superhighway* (New York: McKinsey and Company, 1995); Information Technology Association of America, *Help Wanted: The IT Workforce Gap at the Dawn of a New Century* (Alexandria, VA: Information Technology Association of America, 1997).

59 Ellen Wahl summarizes: "If we consider the situation of women, the problem becomes clear: Among working women, there is still a pay gap. Then there are women on welfare, underemployed, and single-headed households. Technology has the potential to compound the inequitable access to power and economic well-being that girls and women already face." Ellen Wahl, "Access—Four Dimensions," in *Thru the Lens: Women and Information Technology* (Washington, DC: Women and Philanthropy, 1998).

60 Vasilios Makrakis, "Gender and Computing in Schools in Japan: The 'We Can, I Can't' Paradox," *Computers Education* 20 (1993), pp. 191-98.

61 Brunner, "Technology, Gender, and Education."

62 Newton and Beck, "Computing: An Ideal Occupation for Women?"

63 Margolis, "Geek Mythology"; Garnett Foundation, Backyard Project, "Encouraging Young Women to Pursue Careers in Computer Science."

64 Flowers, *Female Educators and Students Assess Gender Equity in Technology Education;* Silvermann, *Guidance, Gender Equity, and Technology Education.*

SELECTED BIBLIOGRAPHY

SELECTED BIBLIOGRAPHY

Anderson, Ronald, and Amy Ronnkvist. "The Presence of Computers in American Schools," in *Teaching, Learning, and Computing: 1998 National Survey,* Center for Research on Information Technology and Organizations (1999) [www.crito.uci.edu/TLC/findings/].

Ayersman, D.J. "Effects of Learning Styles, Programming, and Gender on Computer Anxiety," *Journal of Research on Computing in Education* 28, no. 2 (1995).

Becker, Henry, and Jason Ravitz. "The Equity Threat of Promising Innovations: Pioneering Internet-Connected Schools," *Journal of Educational Computing Research* 19, no. 1 (1998).

Bennett, Dorothy. *Voices of Women in Engineering* (New York: Education Development Center, Center for Children and Technology, 1996).

Beynon, John, and Hugie Mackay, eds. *Computers into Classrooms: More Questions than Answers* (London: Falmer Press, 1993).

Busch, Tor. "Gender, Group Composition, Cooperation, and Self-Efficacy in Computer Studies," *Journal of Educational Computing Research* 14, no. 2 (1997).

Bromley, Hank, and Michael Apple, eds. *Education/Technology/Power: Educational Computing as a Social Practice* (New York: SUNY Press, 1998).

Brunner, Cornelia. "Technology and Gender: Differences in Masculine and Feminine Views," *NASSP Bulletin* 81 (November 1997).

Brunner, Cornelia. "Technology Perceptions by Gender," *Education Digest* 63 (February 1998).

Cassell, Justine, and Henry Jenkins, eds. *From Barbie to Mortal Kombat: Gender and Computer Games* (Cambridge: MIT Press, 1998).

Cherney, Lynn, and Reba Weise, eds. *Wired Women* (Seattle: Seal Press, 1996).

Coley, Richard, et al., Educational Testing Service. *Computers and Classrooms: The Status of Technology in U.S. Schools* (Princeton, NJ: Educational Testing Service, 1996).

Cuban, Larry. "High-Tech Schools and Low-Tech Teaching: A Commentary," *Journal of Computing in Teacher Education* 14, no. 2 (1998).

Dexter, Sara, and Ronald Anderson. "Teachers' Views of Computers as Catalysts for Change in Their Teaching Practice," *Journal of Research on Computing in Education* 31, no. 3 (1999).

Dwyer, David. "Apple Classrooms of Tomorrow: What We've Learned," *Educational Leadership* 51, no. 7 (1996).

Educational Testing Service. *Does It Compute?: The Relationship between Educational Technology and Student Achievement in Mathematics* (Princeton, NJ: ETS, 1998).

Education Week in collaboration with the Milken Exchange on Education Technology. *Technology Counts '99: Building the Digital Curriculum* (Washington, DC: Editorial Projects in Education, 1999).

Furger, Roberta. *Does Jane Compute?: Preserving Our Daughters' Place in the Cyber Revolution* (New York: Warner Books, 1998).

International Society for Technology in Education. *Will New Teachers Be Prepared to Teach in the Digital Age? National Survey on Information Technology in Teacher Education* (Santa Monica, CA: Milken Exchange on Education Technology, 1999).

Kafai, Yasmin. *Minds in Play: Computer Game Design as a Context for Children's Learning* (Hillside, NJ: Lawrence Erlbaum Associates, 1995).

Kafai, Yasmin, and Mitchel Resnick, eds. *Constructionism in Practice: Designing, Thinking and Learning in a Digital World* (Mahwah, NJ: Lawrence Erlbaum Associates, 1996).

Kaiser Family Foundation. *Kids and Media @ the New Millennium: A Comprehensive National Analysis of Children's Media Use* (Menlo Park, CA: Kaiser Family Foundation, 1999).

Klawe, Maria et. al. "Exploring Common Conceptions About Boys and Electronic Games," *The Journal of Computers in Mathematics and Science Teaching* 14, no. 4 (1995).

Kozma, R. and R. Croninger. "Technology and the Fate of At-Risk Students," *Education and Urban Society* 24, no. 4 (1992).

Kramarae, Cheris. ed. *Technology and Women's Voices* (New York: Routledge, 1988).

Linn, Marcia, and Sherry Hsi. *Computers, Teachers, Peers: Science Learning Partners* (Mahwah, NJ: Lawrence Erlbaum Associates, 2000).

Makrakis, Vasilios. "Gender and Computing in Schools in Japan: The 'We Can, I Can't' Paradox," *Computers Education* 20 (1993).

Martin, C. Diane, ed. *In Search of Gender-Free Paradigms for Computer Science* (Washington, DC: International Society for Technology in Education, 1992).

Means, Barbara, ed. *Technology and Education Reform: The Reality Behind the Promise* (San Francisco: Jossey-Bass Publishers, 1994).

National Council for Accreditation of Teacher Education (NCATE), *Technology and the New Professional Teacher* (Washington, DC: NCATE, 1997).

National Research Council, Computer Science and Telecommunications Board. *Being Fluent with Information Technology* (Washington, DC: National Academy Press, 1999).

Pepi, David. "The Emperor's New Computer: A Critical Look at Our Appetite for Computer Technology," *Journal of Teacher Education* 47, no. 3 (1996).

Rosser, Sue. *Re-Engineering Female Friendly Science* Athene Series (New York: Teachers College Press, 1997).

Rosser, Sue. *Teaching the Majority: Breaking the Gender Barrier in Science, Mathematics, and Engineering* (New York: Teachers College Press, 1995).

Rubin, Andee et. al. "What Kinds of Educational Computer Games Would Girls Like?" Paper presented at the American Educational Research Association annual meeting, Boston, April 1997 [www.terc.edu/mathequity/gw/html/MITpaper.html].

Schofield, Janet. *Computers and Classroom Culture* (New York: Cambridge University Press, 1995).

Sutton, Rosemary. "Equity and Computers in the Schools: A Decade of Research." *Review of Educational Research* 61, no. 4 (Winter 1991).

Tarlin, Ellen. "Computers in the Classrooms: Where are All the Girls?" *Harvard Educational Review, Focus Series*, no. 3 (1997).

Turkle, Sherry. *Life on the Screen* (New York: Touchstone, 1997).

Turkle, Sherry. *The Second Self: Computers and the Human Spirit* (New York: Simon and Schuster, 1984).

U.S. Department of Commerce. *Falling through the Net: New Data on the Digital Divide* (Washington, DC: Department of Commerce, 1998).

AAUW EQUITY LIBRARY

Tech-Savvy: Educating Girls in the New Computer Age
Explores girls' and teachers' perspectives of today's computer culture and technology use at school, home, and the workplace. Presents recommendations for broadening access to computers for girls and others who don't fit the "male hacker/computer geek" stereotype. 100 pages/2000.
$11.95 members/$12.95 nonmembers.

Voices of a Generation: Teenage Girls on Sex, School, and Self
Compares the comments of roughly 2,100 girls nationwide on peer pressure, sexuality, the media, and school. The girls were 1997 and 1998 participants in AAUW teen forums called Sister-to-Sister Summits. The report explores differences in girls' responses by race, ethnicity, and age and offers the girls' action proposals to solve common problems. 95 pages/1999.
$13.95 members/ $14.95 nonmembers.

Gaining a Foothold: Women's Transitions Through Work and College
Examines how and why women make changes in their lives through education. The report profiles three groups—women going from high school to college, from high school to work, and from work back to formal education—using both quantitative and qualitative methods. Findings include an analysis of women's educational decisions, aspirations, and barriers. 100 pages/1999.
$11.95 members/ $12.95 nonmembers.

Higher Education in Transition: The Politics and Practices of Equity Symposium Proceedings
A compilation of papers presented at AAUW's June 1999 higher education symposium in Washington, D.C. Topics addressed include campus climate and multiculturalism, higher education faculty and success, higher education student retention and success, and the effect of equity issues on higher education curricula and classrooms. 390 pages/1999.
$19.95 members/$21.95 nonmembers.

Gender Gaps: Where Schools Still Fail Our Children
Measures schools' mixed progress toward gender equity and excellence since the 1992 publication of *How Schools Shortchange Girls*. Report compares student course enrollments, tests, grades, risks, and resiliency by race and class as well as gender. It finds some gains in girls' achievement, some areas where boys—not girls—lag, and some areas, like technology, where needs have not yet been addressed. 150 pages/1998.
$12.95 members/ $13.95 nonmembers.

Gender Gaps Executive Summary
Overview of *Gender Gaps* report with selected findings, tables, bibliography, and recommendations for educators and policy-makers. 24 pages/1998.
$6.95 members/$7.95 nonmembers.

Separated By Sex: A Critical Look at Single-Sex Education for Girls
The foremost educational scholars on single-sex education in grades K–12 compare findings on whether girls learn better apart from boys. The report, including a literature review and a summary of a forum convened by the AAUW Educational Foundation, challenges the popular idea that single-sex education is better for girls than coeducation. 99 pages/1998.
$11.95 AAUW members/$12.95 nonmembers.

Gender and Race on the Campus and in the School: Beyond Affirmative Action Symposium Proceedings
A compilation of papers presented at AAUW's June 1997 college/university symposium in Anaheim, California. Symposium topics include K–12 curricula and student achievement, positive gender and race awareness in elementary and secondary school, campus climate and multiculturalism, higher education student retention and success, and the nexus of race and gender in higher education curricula and classrooms. 428 pages/1997.
$19.95 AAUW members/$21.95 nonmembers.

Girls in the Middle: Working to Succeed in School
Engaging study of middle school girls and the strategies they use to meet the challenges of adolescence. Report links girls' success to school reforms like team teaching and cooperative learning, especially where these are used to address gender issues. 128 pages/1996.
$12.95 AAUW members /$14.95 nonmembers.

Growing Smart: What's Working for Girls in School Executive Summary and Action Guide
Illustrated summary of academic report identifying themes and approaches that promote girls' achievement and healthy development. Based on review of more than 500 studies and reports. Includes action strategies, program resource list, and firsthand accounts of some program participants. 60 pages/1995.
$10.95 AAUW members/$12.95 nonmembers.

How Schools Shortchange Girls: The AAUW Report
Marlowe paperback edition, 1995. A startling examination of how girls are disadvantaged in America's schools, grades K–12. Includes recommendations for educators and policy-makers as well as concrete strategies for change. 240 pages.
$11.95 AAUW members/$12.95 nonmembers.

Hostile Hallways: The AAUW Survey on Sexual Harassment in America's Schools
The first national study of sexual harassment in school, based on the experiences of 1,632 students in grades 8 through 11. Gender and ethnic/racial (African American, Hispanic, and white) data breakdowns included. Commissioned by the AAUW Educational Foundation and conducted by Louis Harris and Associates. 28 pages/1993.
$8.95 AAUW members/$11.95 nonmembers.

SchoolGirls: Young Women, Self-Esteem, and the Confidence Gap
Doubleday, 1994. Riveting book by journalist Peggy Orenstein in association with AAUW shows how girls in two racially and economically diverse California communities suffer the painful plunge in self-esteem documented in *Shortchanging Girls, Shortchanging America*. 384 pages/1994.
$11.95 AAUW members/$12.95 nonmembers.

Shortchanging Girls, Shortchanging America Executive Summary
Summary of the 1991 poll that assesses self-esteem, educational experiences, and career aspirations of girls and boys ages 9–15. Revised edition reviews poll's impact, offers action strategies, and highlights survey results with charts and graphs. 20 pages/1994.
$8.95 AAUW members/$11.95 nonmembers.

AMERICAN
ASSOCIATION OF
UNIVERSITY
WOMEN

Order Form

Name_____ AAUW membership # (if applicable) _____

Street _____

City/State/ZIP _____

Daytime phone (_____)_____ E-mail_____

Item	Price Member/Nonmember	Quantity	Total
Tech-Savvy: Educating Girls in the New Computer Age	$11.95/$12.95	_____	_____
Voices of a Generation	$13.95/$14.95	_____	_____
Gaining a Foothold	$11.95/$12.95	_____	_____
Higher Education in Transition	$19.95/$21.95	_____	_____
Gender Gaps: Where Schools Still Fail Our Children	$12.95/$13.95	_____	_____
Gender Gaps Executive Summary	$6.95/$7.95	_____	_____
Separated By Sex	$11.95/$12.95	_____	_____
Gender and Race on the Campus and in the School	$19.95/$21.95	_____	_____
Girls in the Middle: Working to Succeed in School	$12.95/$14.95	_____	_____
Growing Smart Executive Summary and Action Guide	$10.95/$12.95	_____	_____
How Schools Shortchange Girls	$11.95/$12.95	_____	_____
Hostile Hallways	$8.95/$11.95	_____	_____
SchoolGirls	$11.95/$12.95	_____	_____
Shortchanging Girls Executive Summary	$8.95/$11.95	_____	_____

Subtotal: _____

Sales Tax: _____

Shipping/Handling (see chart below): _____

Total Order ($25 minimum): _____

For bulk pricing on orders of 10 or more, call 800/225-9998 ext. 520.

For rush orders, call 800/225-9998 ext. 520. A $5 fee plus actual shipping charges will apply.

Shipments to foreign countries are sent surface rate and postage is charged at cost plus a $15 handling charge. All applicable duties and taxes are paid by customer.

AAUW Federal Identification Number: 53-0025390.

Shipping and Handling (based on order size)
$25–$49.99 . . . $7.95
$50–$99.99 . . . $8.95
$100–$249.99 . $10.95
$250–$350 . . . . $15.95
Over $350 . . . . $4.95 plus 5% of subtotal

❏ Check/Money Order (Please make payable in U.S. currency to Newton Manufacturing Co. Do not send cash.)

❏ MasterCard/Visa   Card #___ ___ ___ ___ - ___ ___ ___ ___ - ___ ___ ___ ___ - ___ ___ ___ ___ Expiration_____

Name on card _____

Cardholder signature _____

SATISFACTION GUARANTEED: If you are not completely satisfied with your purchase, please return it within 90 days for exchange, credit, or refund. Videos are returnable only if defective, and for replacement only.

FOR MAIL ORDERS, SEND THIS FORM TO:
AAUW Sales Office
Newton Manufacturing Co.
P.O. Box 927
Newton, IA 50208-0927

FOR TELEPHONE ORDERS, CALL:
800/225-9998 ext. 520
800/500-5118 fax

TO ORDER ONLINE:
www.aauw.org